TONY MOORE

Tony Moore is a cultural historian, commentator and documentary film-maker with a special interest in Australian pop culture, artistic bohemia and Labor politics. He is Commissioning Editor of Pluto Press Australia, prior to which he was a program maker at ABC TV where his last documentary was *Bohemian Rhapsody: Rebels of Australian Culture,* now the subject of a PhD he is completing at the University of Sydney. Tony's recent essay on Marcus Clarke, 'Urban Iconoclast', was selected for *Best Essays* 2005, edited by Robert Dessaix and published by Black Inc.

For my parents,
Jean, Eric and Jim,
who taught me to laugh

AUSTRALIAN SCREEN CLASSICS

the barry mckenzie movies

TONY MOORE

AUSTRALIAN FILM COMMISSION
NATIONAL FILM & SOUND ARCHIVE

First published by Currency Press Pty Ltd and the Australian Film Commission in 2005.

Currency Press Pty Ltd
PO Box 2287, Strawberry Hills
NSW 2012 Australia
enquiries@currency.com.au
www.currency.com.au

National Film and Sound Archive
A division of the Australian Film Commission
GPO Box 2002, Canberra
ACT 2601 Australia
www.nfsa.afc.gov.au

Australian Screen Classics series: ISSN 1447-557X

National Library of Australia—Cataloguing-in-Publication Data:

Moore, Tony 1961-
The Barry McKenzie movies.
Bibliography.
ISBN 0 86819 748 3.
1. McKenzie, Barry (Fictitious character). 2. Humphries, Barry, 1934- - Characters - Barry McKenzie. 3. Feature films - Australia - History and criticism. 4. Australian wit and humor. 5. Motion pictures, Australian. I. Title. (Series: Australian screen classics, 1447-557X).
791.4372

Cover design by Kate Florance, Currency Press
Front cover shows Barry McKenzie (Barry Crocker) and Edna Everage (Barry Humphries) in a London 'Black Cab' bound for Earls Court. Photo courtesy of Phillip Adams, sourced from NFSA. Back cover shows Barry McKenzie (Barry Crocker) and then Prime Minster of Australia, Gough Whitlam. Photo supplied courtesy of Grundy Television Pty Ltd.
Typeset by Currency Press in Iowan Old Style roman 9.5 pt.
Printed by Southwood Press, Marrickville

AUSTRALIAN SCREEN CLASSICS

JANE MILLS
Series Editor

Our national cinema plays a vital role in our cultural heritage and in showing us what it is to be Australian. But the picture can be blurred by unruly forces including competing artistic aims, inconstant personal tastes, political vagaries, constantly changing priorities in screen education and training, and technological innovations and market forces.

When these forces remain unconnected, the result can be an artistically impoverished cinema and audiences who are disinclined to seek out and derive pleasure from a diverse range of films.

Screen culture, of which this series is a part, is the glue needed to stick these forces together. It's the plankton in the food chain that feeds the imagination of our filmmakers and their audiences. It's what makes sense of the opinions, memories, responses, knowledge and exchange of ideas about film.

Above all, screen culture is informed by a *love* of cinema. And it has to be carefully nurtured if we are to understand

and appreciate the aesthetic, moral, intellectual and sentient value of our national cinema.

Australian Screen Classics will match some of our best-loved films with some of our most distinguished writers and thinkers, drawn from the worlds of culture, criticism and politics. All we ask of our writers is that they feel passionate about the films they choose. Through these thoughtful, elegantly-written books, we hope that screen culture will work its sticky magic.

Jane Mills is a Senior Research Associate at the Australian Film, Television & Radio School, a Board Member of the Sydney Film Festival and is the recipient of a scholarship at the Centre for Cultural Research, University of Western Australia.

CONTENTS

ACKNOWLEDGMENTS

In writing this book I am indebted to small army of Bazza enthusiasts that include his creators, chroniclers and fans. I particularly want to thank Barry Humphries, Barry Crocker and Phillip Adams for their interest in this project and providing their reminiscences over the years.

A book like this rests on its research, and I gratefully acknowledge the people and institutions that helped me clarify my memories and correct my mistakes: Wendy Borchers at ABC TV archives; Morgan Gregory at the Australian Film Commission; TV historian Andrew Mercado; Kylie Connell at Grundy; Ian Duncan at The Whitlam Institute and the Honourable E.G. Whitlam who took it upon himself to check Hansard for a witty interjection no longer missing in action.

I salute those who fight the good fight to revive Australia's lost film culture: the gang at *Strewth!* magazine for liberating *Barry McKenzie Holds His Own* from archive limbo; Alex Meskovic from the late, lamented Chauvel cinema for generously screening the classic; and Umbrella and their producer Mark Hartley for getting *Holds His Own* and all the extras onto DVD—go out and buy it! I want to express a special note of gratitude to Simon Drake and the team at the National Film and Sound Archive who co-publish *Australian Screen Classics* with Currency Press, and came up with a wealth of images for this book.

Books, like filmmaking, are a collective enterprise. Thanks to friends Chris Mikul and Ed Wright for kindly reading the draft manuscript and their sage suggestions, and to Richard White, my PhD supervisor at the University of Sydney, for disciplining my passions and flights of fancy with a respect for the facts. Thanks to Sam Clarke and Rob Kable for producing a promotional DVD for the book. I want to thank the creative team at Currency Press: Kate Florance for her wonderful designs; Claire Grady for proofing and typesetting and her patience with an author for whom dotting the i is not a natural inclination; Deborah Franco for publicity and Victoria Chance for having faith in me and Bazza. A special thanks must go the editor of this series, Jane Mills, for her guidance, patience, good humour, open mind and incredible knowledge. Jane has a vision for a living, critical cinema culture in this country, and for an ex-pom she certainly knows her Aussie movies.

Audiences are often the missing ingredient in film appreciation. This book is a belated cooee to my old schools mates (and odd teacher) at Port Kembla Primary and Kanahooka High where we honed the obsessive art of movie fandom.

Finally I want to thank my wife, Lizbeth, and children, Joseph and Eliza, for putting up with umpteen viewings of the Barry McKenzie films and for their infinite tolerance as I sat laughing at my lap top, singing 'chunder in the old Pacific Sea'.

Tony Moore, 2005

Illustration acknowledgements

Thank you to the following for permission to reproduce the images on the following pages:

Phillip Adams (sourced from The National Film and Sound Archive), front cover, pages 9, 14, 17, 18, 20, 22, 29, 31, 56, 86.

Umbrella Entertainment page 68.

The photographs on pages 36, 41, 45, 47, 48, 50, 52 and 71 are supplied courtesy of Grundy Television Pty Ltd.

The *Barry McKenzie Holds His Own* DVD is currently available from Umbrella Entertainment. *The Adventures of Barry McKenzie* DVD will be available from Umbrella Entertainment in 2006.
www.umbrellaent.com.au

Introduction

Dinki-di Tales of a True Blue Boy

Struggling to make a living as an actor in pre-swinging 1960s London, a young Australian of bohemian habits accepted a commission to write a comic strip that was to change his life. His name was Barry Humphries, and he had a gift for using humour to skewer his countrymen's foibles. Peter Cook, editor of the satirical magazine *Private Eye,* asked the young expat to aim his barbed wit at the hordes of other young Australians then crowding into the west London neighbourhoods of Earls Court and Notting Hill, and Barry McKenzie, a young, uncouth innocent abroad, was born.

Drawn by New Zealander Nicholas Garland, the cartoon Barry McKenzie looked like a cross between Chesty Bond and the Jolly Swagman, dressed in a 1950s double-breasted suit screwed down with a wide-brimmed Akubra hat that never left his head. 'Bazza', as he was known, was vulgar and irrepressible, perpetually sucking on 'ice cold tubes of Fosters', trying unsuccessfully to get 'a sheila into a game of sink the sausage', and 'chundering' at will on unfortunate 'poms' who crossed his inebriated path. He allowed Humphries to have a spray at

The comic strip Barry McKenzie written by Barry Humphries and drawn by Nicholas Garland for *Private Eye*.

everything he disliked about Australia and England. The strip became a cult hit in Britain. In Australia it was banned. Against the odds it was made into two early films of the 1970s Australian cinema revival, both directed by Bruce Beresford in close collaboration with Humphries.

It's difficult to believe that as a teenager I was allowed to show *Barry McKenzie Holds His Own,* the 1974 sequel to *The Adventures of Barry McKenzie* (1972), at my high school in 1976. Today, with lines like 'our dear little stunted, slant-eyed yellow friends' and 'have a crack at putting the ferret through the furry hoop', it would ring alarm bells. But in the libertarian '70s our teachers knew nothing about political correctness. What we schoolboys knew was that this film, with its ribald humour, inventive Aussie slang, great songs, slapstick, beer, violence, vomiting, vampires, prostitutes and kung-fu fights was a riot. And who could doubt that *Holds His Own* was 'a bloody good cultural show', to quote one of its characters, when the Prime Minister himself, Gough Whitlam, made an appearance? As the years have passed both Barry McKenzie movies have, like a fine brew, only got better.

I first encountered Barry McKenzie as an icon of a cocky, cheeky Aussie pop culture that was flowing through the suburbs in the '70s. If the films allowed Humphries and Beresford to play with memories of a disappearing Australia of their youth and to pit the certainties of the old Australia against the pretensions of the new, they provided my generation with a way of making sense of social changes we were living through—and rather liked. By the early '70s the transgressive values of the late 1960s cultural revolution were going feral in the back blocks of Australia. The permissive society may have been hatched in the kaftans of the counter-culture but its ground zero was in the suburbs.

For teenagers in the '70s, pop culture was a smorgasbord of 'tubes, boobs and pubes'—thanks in no small part to the cultural iconoclasts of the '60s getting their hands on the mainstream media. From the cartoon surfy pig *Captain Goodvibes* to the surreal comedy *Aunty Jack*, to glam pop band Skyhooks, and to sex symbol Abigail, the Australian airwaves were full of people behaving badly. From the time I was 10, sizzling soapie *Number 96* was the hearth around which our family gathered nightly. If adults ceased to be shocked, a generation of children really didn't know what that word meant as they became accustomed to sensation, surprise and difference. What is hard to grasp for older people who struggled against the 1950s cultural cringe, is just how familiarised our generation was to Australian sights and sounds—on the box, at the flicks, over the 'tranny'.

Barry McKenzie seeped into my schoolboy consciousness thanks to the promotional blitz that accompanied the first film. Its theme song, performed by Smacka Fitzgibbon, a leagues club crooner with the nasal drawl of a race caller, combined a jaunty pub sing-a-long with an operatic serenading of the hero with lines like 'from the team that gave you Sir Robert Menzies' and, more amusing for young boys, 'If you want to get your sister in a frenzy, introduce her to Barry McKenzie'. As far as we were concerned its 'R' classification stood for 'rude'—earned, so the rumours went, for vomiting, urinating and dirty language. This was music to schoolboys' ears even if for all those under 18, the film would have to remain an alluring yet unattainable mystery, forbidden fruit, like alcohol and sex.

Hot on the heels of the Bazza song came another version, this time about Gough Whitlam. Again crooned by Smacka, it boasted lines like 'he's a handsome wild colonial man, but he'll join the bloody world if he possibly can'. It aired on the iconoclastic current affairs show *This Day Tonight*, and was sung with gusto by me and my mates in the Port Kembla primary playground. From that moment, in my mind, Barry McKenzie and Gough Whitlam were inextricably connected. Whitlam, like Bazza, was a larger than life Aussie original who had arrived with an all-singing celebrity chorus declaring 'It's Time' and could always surprise when he opened his mouth. Some of the old blokes who hung around Whitlam, like our local member, Rex Connor, wore hats and suits like Bazza and sounded very old Australian, like a cement mixer full of gravel. Bazza stuck it up the poms, and for us 'Aussies' who had to endure taunts from our 'wog' classmates about our second-hand monarch, Bazza and Gough were our home-grown heroes.

I finally saw my first Bazza movie, the M-rated sequel, in 1975 when I was 13. Humphries may have been an urbane aesthete but he was no slouch when it came to self-promotion and the film's producer, Reg Grundy, spared no marketing expense.[1] A merchandising bonanza was unleashed, making the impending Aussie film seem more valid, more like a Hollywood one. Almost three years before *Star Wars* (1977), the marketing strategy was remarkably prescient at courting the youth demographic with the Barry McKenzie drinking songs LP, a comic booklet, posters and a pocket postcard glossary of Bazza-isms that became an instant schoolyard collectible. Adolescent boys the country over began to 'point Percy at the porcelain'. I don't recall any Australian filmmakers since rivalling the Bazza merchandising juggernaut.

A year earlier my family had swapped gritty salami and moussaka Port Kembla for white bread Dapto just a few miles west, an expanding suburban sprawl whose growth was fuelled by 'ten pound poms'. This heightened the relevance for me of Bazza's love/hate relationship with the English. Bazza allowed me to hold my own as an Australian against the pride the Brits could take in Benny Hill, Monty Python and the Goodies. While I was hostile to an imagined and distant English snobbery personified in the royal family, my schoolmates from the industrial North and Midlands were an eccentric, cheeky lot, more bonny than born to rule.

Rather than feeling inferior to these children from the 'mother country', as the middle classes of Humphries' Melbourne suburb of Camberwell might to an imagined Mother Country, I felt that their start in life had been stunted by the English class system. In Australia, these kids tasted the freedom of space, opportunity and mobility, and wanted more of it. In sunny suburban Australia they acquired sun tans, broadened their vowels, and were 'naturalised' into 'Aussies' in a silly but important school boy ritual where they swore allegiance to ocker values over a feast of potato scallops and a vanilla milkshake from a Greek milk bar. From the perspective of a working class childhood in the '70s, Australia really did seem to be 'the greatest little country in the world, no risk', as Bazza had it. Unlike McKenzie's creators, we had not grown up oppressed by a cultural cringe but rather, like Bazza himself, felt sorry for the poor old poms.

Despite the filmmakers' mockery of many of my countrymen's attributes, *Holds His Own* made me, in the words of its fictitious Minister for Culture (played by Humphries) who introduces the 'fillum', 'proud to be Australian'. It cemented for me the idea that any Australian patriotism should be, first and foremost, based on taking the piss, of laughing not just at one's self but at the powerful, whether they be upper class Brits, or the PM himself. The finale in *Holds His Own,* where Gough welcomes Bazza home and ad libs 'Arise Dame Edna', elicited a spontaneous roar of approval from the audience. Frequently recycled in montage tributes, this topsy-turvy assumption of royal prerogatives created one of the era's enduring symbols. Whitlam was dismissed the following November and his tragic clash with vice-regal authority turned me and many of my mates into schoolboy republicans. Not surprisingly, along with Maoist Blinky Bill T-shirts and Eureka stockade flags, Bazza became a weapon in our teenage political rebellion during the dreary Fraser years.

The two Barry McKenzie films became cult objects of

veneration among die-hard fans like me. In Australia the mutation from hit to cultdom occurs because of the tendency of mainstream taste-makers to forget our films after the first blush of hype, leaving old movies to secret dissection in alternative cinemas and on video. But if fans can keep them alive and reveal meanings that speak to new audiences then they just might become classics. Today I consider these films to be two of the funniest comedies ever made in Australia. But they are much more than this. By fusing critical ideas from the artistic fringe with cherished local traditions, Humphries and Beresford created something recognisably Australian yet entirely new and surprising.

Humphries is a contradictory artist. An aesthete attracted to 'decadents' and dandies like James McNeill Whistler, Oscar Wilde and the Australian painter Charles Conder, he is intrigued by low life and vulgarity. A sophisticate who despairs of suburbia, Humphries' comedy revels in parodying the prejudices and ignorant certainties of old white Australia. He eschewed the modernist pretensions of a Patrick White for the roar of the crowd, appealing to popular taste via the mass media. An abstinent alcoholic, he made a film in which beer is the elixir of life. A bohemian, he adopts the mask of the ocker.

Beresford was a young Sydney filmmaker who had cut his teeth on underground shorts and had made films in Africa and London before landing a job running the Experimental Film Fund of the prestigious British Film Institute—not bad for a scruffy long-haired colonial. He met Humphries in London in 1967 and found that they laughed at the same things. The zeal of European experimental cinema did not affect Beresford's Sydney bullshit antenna and he happily produced a mock 'underground film' for Humphries' one-man show in the late 1960s.[2] What Beresford liked about the Bazza comic strip was 'Humphries' unpredictable and pointed satire ... and his ear for the vagaries and vulgarity of Australian English'.[3] In 1968 Beresford first suggested to Humphries that they make a feature film from the comic but agreed it would only have legs if they found the perfect lead actor to fill Bazza's wobbly boots.

In 1969 Humphries excitedly rang Beresford to tell him he'd met a singer 'with a great big chin'.[4] And in crooner, cabaret artist and popular TV personality, Barry Crocker, Barry McKenzie came to life. As host of the *Sound of Music* variety TV program, Crocker was about as Bazza-like as Julie Andrews. But once the McKenzie hat was on, Crocker became Bazza right down to the jutting jaw and foul mouth. Unbeknown to his blue-rinse fans, Crocker had kicked off his career doing 'blue' jokes and drinking songs in the tough licensed clubs of Western Sydney. With his trained baritone voice, Crocker could not only sing the dirty ditties in the script but also hold and entertain a crowd. Beresford admired the easy charm and basic innocence he brought to Bazza as 'it enabled us to get away with some of Humphries' most scandalous euphemisms'.[5] Crocker gave Barry McKenzie a new quality—charisma.

The final important ingredient was producer Phillip Adams, a catalyst in the resurrection of the local film industry in the late 1960s and who helped set up the Australian Film Development Corporation (AFDC), the government film bank. Adams was a man of refined and popular tastes who combined socialist politics with a day job as an ad man and a column in Rupert Murdoch's paper, the *Australian*. With a keen enthusiasm for larrikin humour, the rich inheritance of a poor childhood

Barry Crocker gave Barry McKenzie a new quality—charisma.

in suburban Melbourne, Adams was a doer. He navigated the film through the AFDC maze and lent the project his considerable organisational and promotional talents. *Adventures* went into production in London in January 1972 with a budget of $250,000 drawn entirely from the Australian government. It was a tiny sum even by the standards of the time but was compensated for with a polished script, good comic acting, and a skilled and imaginative young crew that included Director of Photography Don McAlpine, film editors William Anderson and John Scott, and Peter Best on musical score.[6] Invested with the hopes of Canberra's cultural commissars of reviving a local film industry, Barry McKenzie had gone from smuggled contraband to national flagship in a matter of years.

The movie was a commercial smash, earning $330,000 and showing that Australian films could not only hold their own at the box office against Hollywood and British flicks but actually turn a healthy profit.[7] It also did well in the UK, where it broke the records for any Australian film to date. The Fosters-drenched film became an export lager.

Critics then and since have been divided. For some, the film's very commercial success condemned it as low entertainment aimed at the masses. Conservatives were duly outraged. What would people overseas think of Australia now? The *Age* fretted that such a film 'would only serve to confirm the world's suspicions that we are a *Wake in Fright* nation of Bazzas and Storks'.[8] Modernist artists and critics from an earlier generation, notably the ubiquitous cultural commentator Max Harris, despaired that they had fought for cosmopolitanism only to have these philistine 'ockers' drag Australian sophistication back into the 6 o'clock swill:

> We thought we had won the battle in the decades since the 1940s. But clearly we lost the war ... Now we're back where we started. Mr Adams, Bob Hawke, Barry Humphries et al have taken advantage of the so-called new nationalism ... Ocker is celebrated. Ocker is phoenix. Ocker is King.[9]

The convict streak was exposed to the world like a grimy stain on the national underpants.

The Barry McKenzie films are not especially cherished by cinephiles who look to the visual art of filmmaking. Nor do they deliver symbolic or hidden meanings to those who like complex layering in their films. Both films are full of meaning but those messages are on the surface, sign-posted in dialogue and action. It is pointless to criticise the Bazza films for what they are not and far more rewarding to appreciate them for what they are—accomplished, visceral and subversive comedy with a great deal to say about Australia.

Their significance stems in part from the time and place in which they were created. They were emblematic of the so-called 'New Nationalism' associated with the Whitlam era, and of the 'Ocker cinema' that kicked-off the new wave of Australian cinema. Bazza, his 'one-eyed trouser snake' at the ready, also played his part in the permissive 'sex 'n sin' atmosphere of the early '70s media. *Adventures* was a leading boundary breaker, helping to free up what could be said and shown in our public art. But the films should not be framed simply as '70s nostalgia, nor as the awkward adolescent stage of the Australian film industry. They're important because they deal with key tensions in Australian culture, between the province and the metropolitan centre, the bohemian artist and the working class larrikin, the wowser and the libertine, authority and unruliness, cosmopolitanism and white Australia, the cultivated versus the philistine. In a period of rapid social transformation, Humphries and Beresford used the ocker mask of Bazza to make controversial comments on class, masculinity, sex, race, religion, art and politics. Watching the movies today you cannot help but be reminded how little some things have really changed, how the paradoxes of our national life remain unreconciled. But then again, I shouldn't be too critical, as Bazza reminds his English hosts:

> You poor old poms don't know what you're missing. Beaut sandy beaches, lovely juicy steaks, big shiny cars, millions of drive-in bottle shops, decent church-going buggers all over the place and gorgeous clean-living sheilas who root like rattlesnakes!

To grumble in the face of such endowments would be plain un-Australian. As long as we can produce a bullshit detector like Barry McKenzie all is not lost.

1

The Adventures of Barry McKenzie

The Adventures of Barry McKenzie begins in Sydney with the reading of Barry's father's will that decrees the son will only inherit if he returns to England to absorb the culture of the mother country. With his fussy Aunty Edna (Barry Humphries) as chaperone, Barry, festooned with cameras and a Qantas bag, boards the national carrier bound for London. He discovers a bleak and Dickensian England of squalid lodgings, down-cast immigrants and rapacious hustlers. Beresford favoured shooting London exteriors on overcast days, and took care to have garbage strewn on the streetscape to create a grey *mise en scène* that played up to the Australian prejudice of miserable weather and decay. Once ensconced in the Australian ghetto of Earls Court with his mate Curly (Paul Bertram) and bibulous expats (notably a lairish cameo by Beresford) and a steady supply of foaming Fosters, Barry has a succession of encounters with English men and women who alternatively want to fleece, promote, exploit, shag, marry, psychoanalyse, arrest or fight him (and occasionally several of these at once).

For his part, Barry considers most of the natives to be either

An innocent abroad: Barry McKenzie arrives in Earls Court.

'pommy bastards', or 'poofs' and frequently both. Though the 'potato peelers' (sheilas) are fair game for 'a knee trembler', Bazza fears that they 'don't like it plain and simple', and his sexual inexperience leads him from one amorous misadventure to another. Despite all his linguistic sexual bravado, Barry is a virgin, and will remain one. Ever the incorrigible ocker, Barry continually misreads the social signals to great comic effect but is also game for new experiences that invariably lead him into trouble. Our hero leaves mounting chaos in his wake, climaxing in the exposure of his 'old fella' live on a BBC TV program about the artistic renaissance in Australia.

The film is episodic, a loosely connected series of standout sketches in the manner of the comic strip from which it came. Beresford, who confessed to only ever liking three comic strips himself, *Prince Valiant, Doonesbury* and *Barry McKenzie,* happily admits sitting down with the comics and lifting 'scenes, characters and dialogue for the film script'. This narrative structure has a fine pedigree in the literary genre of the picaresque. *The Adventures of Barry McKenzie* echoes the eighteenth century novels *Tom Jones* and *Moll Flanders* where a young hero sets out into the wide world to encounter a passing parade of eccentrics, villains, misfortunes and, of course, sexual adventures—all of which have their origins in the very origins of the novel: Cervantes' seventeenth century Spanish masterpiece, *Don Quixote*.

Much of the humour in *Adventures* comes from the effortless way the charming but vulgar Bazza moves up and down the British social register, mixing with upper class fops, trendy TV producers, home county Tories, Eastend gangsters, a Jewish psychiatrist and hippies. These characters are presented as English grotesques and are played by a who's who of British comedy—for laughs but also to showcase some of the baser elements of human nature and contemporary social malaise that Humphries disdained. The counterpoint to this exotic menagerie is the Australian monstrosity Edna Everage, safe and smug in her suburban carapace.

Spike Milligan plays the oily, nameless slum landlord who is all but covered in cobwebs. He leads Bazza past prostitutes and ne'er-do-wells to a dog box that requires a pound note in a meter just to keep the light running. Of all the characters Barry meets it is the Gorts, an in-bred, inward-looking family of Tory dysfunctionals, who take the cake. Mrs Gort (Avice Landon) looks like the Queen but is actually a glimpse into the Thatcherite future. A social climbing 'Little Englander' chauvinist, she disinfects her mail because the postman is black, has a Winston Churchill figurine mug, and pretends she has a cook. She assumes that Barry is one of 'those wealthy Australian shareholders' and plots to marry him off to her put-upon, thumb-sucking Young Conservative daughter, Sarah (Jenny Tomasin). The balding, tweedy hubby Ronald (played by Ealing Film stalwart Dennis Price) is a panting masochist who dresses up as a schoolboy and tries to persuade Barry to discipline him.

If Humphries thought little of philistine conservatives he thought even less of hippies. A trio of alternative musos who claim to 'just roam around the country making the simple, unaffected music working people like' are revealed to be greedy, violent, Machiavellian fame-fuckers. Their leader, Hoot (Barry Humphries), is an American accented hippy conman who wants to exploit Barry's musical talents and hisses things like 'if we can't make bread out of an authentic Australian folk singer I'll get out of this racket'. Hospitalised following a brawl, Bazza falls into the clutches of another inspired grotesque, Jewish shrink Dr de Lamphrey (Humphries again) who is an amalgam of the psychiatrists Humphries was forced to endure while confined to various sanitaria for his drinking problems and depression in the late 1960s. While Bazza is strapped to a table like Frankenstein's monster, de Lamphrey scuttles around the floor trying to decipher his patient's exotic argot and asking whether he can see patterns in the carpet until a 'technicolour yawn' stops him in his tracks. When Barry visits Leslie (Mary Anne Severne), a young family friend, he mistakes her suave, suit-wearing lesbian lover Claude (Judith Furse) for a man. Ironically, she is the most gentleman-like person England has yet thrown at Barry. But Claude is also a bit of a lech, and can't keep her wandering eye off Barry's aunty.

Presiding over this freak show is, of course, the Moonee Ponds monster, Edna Everage, familiar to Australian audiences from her appearances on stage and TV throughout the 1960s. She is a pantomime suburban housewife with garish make-up and clothes and frightening in her smothering respectability and philistinism. It was Beresford who insisted that Edna—who had nothing to do with the comic strip—be catapulted

English grotesques: Barry and Edna Everage (Barry Humphries) visit the Gort family.

into the movie, and it was an inspired decision. She is a dominant but not unappealing character throughout both films, and the only person who can bring Barry to heel. In a topsy-turvy conceit Edna alternately nags and mollycoddles her strapping nephew as if he were a small child. The subtext is transparent: Australian men never grow up and need looking after by mother figures, whether they be actual mothers, or wives or, in Bazza's case, aunties. Given that Humphries was a boy during the war it may well have seemed to him that women rule the roost. If, as some film theorists think, this castration anxiety on the part of post-war men gave America the femmes

Hard-boiled housewife Edna Everage (Barry Humphries) warns Barry to behave.

fatale of film noir, then it gave Australia Edna Everage.

The Edna of the Bazza films is a very different woman to the celebrity megastar of today. Back then she was the same housewife Australian audiences had first met in 1956 when she appeared on TV at its birth as a volunteer Olympics hostess, driving an official to apopolexy as she primly rejected all nationalities offered as billets for her Moonee Ponds home. By the early '70s her dress is inappropriately lairy for a woman of her age. Unlike most of the discrete English women she meets, Edna is over the top and forever intruding. Like Bazza, she has no sex life, lamenting her husband Norm's prostrate operation. But as an Aunty she finds consolation in doting on Barry, cooking lamingtons for him and his mates. As well as keeping an eye on her nephew, she hopes to take in 'the olde worlde charm' of England but is condescending about the standard of British amenities. For Edna, England has never recovered from the blitz and so she hands out parcels of dripping as her family had during the (fictitious) 'Fat for Britain Drive'. Edna is a constant reminder that no matter how cosmopolitan their adventures, the cloying, philistine suburbs are never far away. Except that, throughout the Bazza movies, Edna's metamorphosis into a smart-mouthed dame with a good line in put-downs is well under way. She may be a housewife but she's also hard boiled, like a baited lolly.[10]

Humphries recently described Bazza as 'an innocent adrift treading bravely the moral quicksands of the swinging London of his day'.[11] *Adventures* follows in the tradition of Voltaire's *Candide* and fish-out-of-water films like *Mr Smith Goes to Washington* (1939) and *Ninotchka* (1939), playing with the tensions and misunderstandings between provincial hicks and the metropolis. An Australian film precursor was Ken Hall's comedy, *It Isn't Done* (1937) in which a humble farmer (Cecil Kellaway) inherits a baronial estate and moves the family to England, to the chagrin of the neighbouring aristocrats. An obvious successor is *Crocodile Dundee* (1986). The corruption of the innocent is a popular theme in Australian memoirs and many, including Humphries' own autobiography, *More Please*, recycle this trope, in which a young man from the provinces or the suburbs is inducted into the secrets of the bohemian demimonde. But whereas the heroes in these rites of passage stories discover the mysteries of the metropolis through sex, Barry's desires are continually frustrated, his growth to manhood stunted by sexual dysfunction and emotional Peter Panism.

Like many frustrated men, Barry never stops talking about sex but it's the sex talk of schoolyard braggers, amusing coming from a six-foot bloke. Because of his awkwardness with women, his fumbled liaisons always end in farce. When a vacuous and buxom blonde actress named Caroline Thighs (Maria O'Brien) throws herself at Barry he gets it all wrong after consulting the *Karma Sutra*. Unable to find a herbal aphrodisiac at the local Indian grocery store he anoints his loins in curried beef with

'Pommy sheilas don't like it plain and simple.' Virgin Barry McKenzie in bed with Caroline Thights (Maria O'Brien).

disastrous results. After leaving a Young Conservative dance early with the comely Sarah Gort, he is unable to make the first move, even though one of his mates (played by a young John Clarke) advises him that 'some of those sheilas that don't look so hot are great little performers'. His pursuit of hippy waif Blanche (Julie Covington) ends in a rumble as her jealous switch blade-wielding boyfriend goes for Barry's gonads. Gobsmacked by the feminine vision of Leslie when she frocks up to elude the police, the gauche Bazza is moved to declare 'Kiss my bum if that sheila wouldn't bang like a dunny door', and cops a well deserved slap across the face. McKenzie ends the film as he began it, a boy untouched by amorous hands, snug in his auntie's embrace.

Adventures defies easy pigeon-holing as just a shallow 'ocker comedy'. Its creators set out to critique society and shock audiences while producing a commercial success. The filmmakers had served their apprenticeships within the artistic bohemian fringe in Australia and Britain but by the 1970s they wanted to entertain mainstream audiences. Humphries had already tasted success as a performer and Beresford had had his fill of underground filmmaking purity when commissioning at the BFI. They were not the first Australian artists to combine bohemian identities and tastes with careers in the entertainment industry and nor would they be the last. The most entertaining art comes from a cross fertilization of the margins and the mainstream, and this is what makes this film so interesting for me.

Humphries' theatrical experiences in the 1960s had been diverse and they make a deep impression on the film. His early talent for humorous monologues had been nurtured in revue comedy at universities and companies like the Phillip Street Revue in Sydney. At London's alternative Establishment Club in the early 1960s Humphries began to absorb the mood of Britain's cerebral comedy boom. The intellectual side of Humphries' humour is apparent in the film's play with issues like art, Australian identity, expatriation and sexual diversity. Threaded through the beer and chunder are cultural references for those in the know. Barry Crocker recounts sitting through *Adventures* with a guffawing Germaine Greer, who had to explain to him arcane lesbian and literary allusions.[12] It's not, however, an obsession with matters of the mind for which *Adventures* is best remembered.

Humphries had long sought to make an art form of bodily excretions. His one-man shows in the '60s increasingly trod the same fine line between the salon and the toilet that would characterise *Adventures*. What gave the film an edge was an enthusiasm to transgress mainstream middle class taste born out of Humphries' experiments with dada and surrealism and

'I was as dry as a dead dingo's donger.' Bazza downs a cleansing ale with expat mate Curly (Paul Bertram).

Beresford's underground film work. Humphries had exhibited art works like 'Pus in Boots' (a boot filled with custard) and pretended to throw up on trams using homemade vomit. One of Beresford's earliest filmmaking experiences was as cinematographer on the student avant-garde short, *It Droppeth as the Gentle Rain,* which climaxes in the cast being showered in shit from the heavens.[13] Both artists found that playing with the appetites and ablutions of the body could be liberating in a society emerging from a prim postwar conservatism.

You cannot avoid Bazza's sheer physicality. Slave to his appetites, he continually sucks tubes of Fosters, showers himself and his mates in foaming geysers that ejaculate from the cans, and crams lamingtons into his mouth. When he vomits on Dr de Lamphrey, a truly gross and realistic expulsion pours from Barry's gob and trickles down the face of the hapless shrink.[14] Defending his determination to make cinematic history with this graphic 'chunder', Humphries insisted: 'If you don't go over the hill, you'll never know what's on the other side.'[15] When BBC arts host Joan Bakewell (playing herself) responds to Barry's drunken raving with the question 'I don't quite see your point' it's natural for him to stand on his chair, and 'unbutton the mutton'. Just as we think the willy waving can go no further, Barry's drunken mates start putting out a studio fire by urinating on the flames, passing Fosters up a conga line of guzzling human hydrants—thereby indulging two of their greatest pleasures, getting pissed and pissing, literally, on the British cultural establishment. Barry is equally obsessed with his sexual appetites, telling anyone who'll listen that he is about to 'dip the wick', or how he could be up there 'like a rat up a drainpipe'. A crude obsession with genital contact takes the place of romance. Sadly, however, Barry's sex life is rooted in word play rather than foreplay.

Beresford later recalled that McKenzie's 'scatological remarks and euphemisms for bodily excretions and fornication were a source of wonder'.[16] He refers to his penis variously as 'Percy', 'the wife's best friend', and the 'beef bayonet'. Spewing could be 'chunder', 'technicolour yawn', 'parking the tiger' or 'crying

Ruth' (have a go yelling it). In one scene Barry completely bamboozles the bemused locals when he tells them he needs to 'Rinse the Prince? Shake hands with the wife's best friend? Splash the boots?' They stare bewildered as Bazza persists: 'Drain the dragon? Wring the rattle snake? Water the horses? Strain the potatoes? Hang out with big nobs?' Finally the penny drops and someone helpfully suggests 'I think he wants to go to the loo'.

Some of Bazza's vernacular was authentic, picked up by Humphries from his builder father's labourers, in the school playground and in the pubs of Melbourne and Sydney. 'It was marvellously liberating', Humphries recalled, 'to lift slang from C.J. Dennis, Geelong Grammar, Bluey and Curly, the mural felicities of divers memorable dunnies...'[17] He particularly recalled from childhood a hefty tradesman informing his mates he 'was off to strain the potatoes'.[18] But no actual Australian could surpass Barry McKenzie. Humphries happily admitted to topping up 'our seemingly inexhaustible reservoirs of slang' for bodily functions by coining 'quaintly indecent neologisms ... so that the whole thing became an intriguing verbal pastiche of the real and the grotesquely imaginary'.[19] Phrases like 'busy as a one-armed Sydney cab driver with crabs', and 'point Percy at the porcelain' were Humphries originals. Nevertheless, Barry McKenzie's four letter words never get worse than 'shit'. Why use unimaginative words like 'fuck' when you can say 'in up to the apricots and off like a grenade'? Beresford boasts that Bazza is never merely crude, never uses a phrase 'devoid of wit', and that '[t]here is always some striking imagery in the way McKenzie speaks, some astonishing simile or synonym'.[20]

Like football players, drinking mates and old soldiers, Bazza is partial to a 'dirty ditty'. Crocker's two musical numbers are important for the film's sense of fun and allow McKenzie a domain in which he prevails over his detractors. Humphries says he encouraged the 'musical' aspect of the McKenzie films because 'I like shows with songs in them'.[21] Humphries had made his theatrical reputation playing Fagin in the very mainstream musical *Oliver* in London's West End and on Broadway in the mid 1960s, and something of the classic musical was incorporated into *Adventures.* He had written an embryonic Bazza musical while picking a pocket or two in *Oliver*, and it was from this document that Beresford filched one of the film's sing-a-long numbers. Cadging a lift to London with the combie van of musical hippies who call themselves 'The Disciples', Bazza picks up a guitar and launches into an impromptu performance about his favourite obsession:

> I have a little creature
> I guess you can call him a pet
> If there's something wrong with him
> I don't have to call the vet
> He goes everywhere I do
> Whether sleeping or awake
> God ever help me if I lose me little one eyed trouser snake
> Oh me one eyed trouser snake, oh me one eyed trouser snake.

Is this emphasis on body parts and excretions just bad taste to pull in the masses or is there more going on? On one reading of the film Barry McKenzie is a boorish oaf used by Humphries to show his disdain for working class Australians. Certainly Humphries considered too many of his fellow Australians incurably philistine, parochial and vulgar, and had no special love for proletarians. But that wasn't how we read it in working class Dapto. Barry McKenzie was greeted as a celebration of the '70s Aussie Everyman, the Ocker, and seen as a working class hero. Why? Having lived in communities where we used bawdiness, rowdiness and irreverence as weapons against those who would unfairly seek to condescend or control, I've always been attracted to this anti-establishment element in *Adventures*. We rooted for Bazza as he gave the snobs and poseurs an ear or eyeful because we recognised his larrikinism as a form of rebellion.[22]

This form of dissent has deep roots in Australia's folk memory. Outwardly funny, larrikinism is also a bit dangerous as suggested by the original larrikins, working class delinquent youths who disturbed the peace of city streets from the 1870s into the early decades of the twentieth century. The focus of a conservative moral panic in the late nineteenth century, larrikinism also came to be admired by artistic and political libertines as a marker for non-conformity, earthy humour and disdain for authority. The larrikin streak was found in the journalism, bush ballads, jokes and cartoons of the *Bulletin* in the 1890s and shapes how we think of Ned Kelly and the Anzacs. Between the wars, larrikinism typified the big city tabloid sensationalism of *Smith's Weekly* and the comedy of popular humourists.[23] Larrikin libertarianism was strong in the two bohemian subcultures of the late 1950s and '60s through which the young Humphries and Beresford moved, the Melbourne Drift and the Sydney Push. The filmmakers knew the lineage well, as Adams explained:

> I always thought we had a rich tradition of larrikin irreverence that manifests itself in Henry Lawson's *Loaded Dog*, Rene's Mo McCackie and Paul Hogan, in pollies like Bob Hawke and Paul Keating, a constant in which Bazza was but one expression.[24]

The earthy Australian larrikinism in these movies has equivalents in many different folk cultures and art forms, and has been celebrated in recent times under the banner of the 'carnivalesque'. This term is used by literary academics to refer to a topsy-turvy spirit of riotous festivity, famously unleashed in the carnivals of Europe in the fifteenth and sixteenth centuries, in which the lower orders deployed misrule, play, humour and vulgarity to subvert authority and best their betters—if only temporarily. For Soviet literary theorist Mikhail Bakhtin the carnivalesque was a way of understanding a style of dissent that was evident in the literature of Rabelais, and stretched back through the ritualised chaos of the renaissance carnivals to the Roman Saturnalia. Carnivalesque elements in *Adventures* include drunkenness, gluttony, parody, sexual ribaldry, gender confusion, riot and the grotesque. While it was more safety valve than revolution, Bakhtin argued that carnival nevertheless had the potential to make the rulers squirm with discomfort by ridiculing the mystique of power. He must have been on to something because Stalin exiled him to Kazakstan.

Internationally the carnivalesque was in the air during the 1960s and 1970s. It was translated to cinema in Pier Paolo Pasolini's bawdy adaptations of Boccacio's *The Decameron* (1970) and Chaucer's *The Canterbury Tales* (1972). These controversial films pitted an earthy, libertine delight in bodily functions and pleasure, especially sex, against authority figures. Simultaneously in Britain an ancestral fondness for the nudge-nudge, wink-wink, saucy seaside postcard aesthetic was being reinvented in the *Carry On* films and by popular television comedians such as Dick Emery and Benny Hill. Their sexual farce, lavatory laughs and double entendres were foils against starched shirts and uptight bosses. The modernised larrikin carnivalesque had its dress rehearsal in Australian cinema in Tim Burstall's film version of David Williamson's play *Stork* (1971), which also placed an incorrigible and unruly larrikin in an environment where social faux pas became social critique. But Humphries and Beresford took the socio-larrikin genre in new and unexpected directions, cutting across conventional political binaries.

Barry McKenzie is a foil against snobbery and hypocrisy, whether practiced overtly by the English ruling class or, more subtly, by the counter-culture, media professionals and officious state functionaries. Humphries and Beresford shake a well-aimed Fosters at the sacred cows of both the right and the left of Australia in the early 1970s. *Adventures* remains funny not just because so many of the cows are still grazing in our cultural paddock, but because the stand-off between an arrogant, complacent elitism, and an uncontrollable, democratic larrikinism are perennials in Australia's creative and political life. In this struggle I'm unashamedly on the side of Bazza and believe the film's hostility to power and position makes it radical and life affirming, unlike those left wing detractors who find much of Humphries' work conservative and misanthropic.[25]

This theme of liberation can be illustrated by my favourite episode in the film, a public musical performance by Barry at a 'happening' before a large mob of hippies, assorted rockers, even a hip clergyman, gathered in an underground vault reminiscent of Liverpool's Cavern Club.[26] Introduced as an 'Australian folk singer' whose lyrics are 'urgent', Bazza stumbles through an awkward joke to a stony silence. But then, as he starts to explain the historical genesis of the word 'chunder' in his inventive lingo to the assembled counter-culture types, they laugh. Convicts, dispatched to Australia 'for eating a loaf of bread or a hanky', he tells them, would get sea sick on the voyage out, and before hurling over the side of the ship would yell 'watchunder' so 'no poor devil would cop a steaming eyeful'.

'If I can't make some bread out of an authentic Australian folk singer I'll get out of this racket.' Barry Humphries as hippy muso Hoot.

Dedicating his song to the 'chundering founders' of Australia 'the greatest little country in the world, no risk', Barry launches into the 'Old Pacific Sea':

> I was down by Bondi Pier
> Cracking tubes of ice cold beer
> With a bucket full of prawns upon me knee
> When I swallowed the last prawn
> I had a technicolour yawn
> And I chundered in the old Pacific sea

Electric guitars jangle in as the band get hip to the Bazza beat. By the time he gets to the rousing chorus the audience have gone wild and are singing along to 'Drink it up, Drink it up, Crack another dozen prawns and tubes with me'.

In this earnest, 'underground' scene the crude drinking song, performed with gusto by Crocker, transforms these poseurs to spontaneous rapture—something their own 'urgent' and 'relevant' music could not. Watching the movie as an Australian, the moment when the crowd joins in is better than when the audience at the Salzburg folk festival sing along to Edelweiss with Captain Von Trapp. Performance episodes like these occur in both Barry McKenzie films, underscoring those moments where the unaffected yahoo from the colonies gets the better of the supposed sophisticates of the metropolis.

The mixing and mocking of cultural hierarchies like good and bad taste, the solemn and profane, is another carnivalesque gesture, evident in much of Humphries work. The combination of arts broadcasting and urination by Barry's 'piss-artist' mates, for example, is typical of the film's topsy-turvy approach to rarefied bourgeois culture. Barry's crude and chaotic path is entangled with people working in the creative arts—TV producers, ad men, folk singers, and even an avant-garde painter (John Clarke again) unable to resist Barry's charms. The clash of cultures allows the filmmakers to apply the bullshit detector to artistic vogues. Cultural snobs who dismiss *Adventures* as crass, misread the creative values of so-called 'low' art, and may feel threatened by the film's attack on the solemnity of 'high' art pretensions.

The carnivalesque treatment of sexuality in *Adventures* goes beyond the raunchy romps popular in early '70s comedies to

'I don't quite see your point.' Bazza interviewed on BBC TV while artists look on.

explore the farce of sexual incompetence and ambiguity. After 'poms', Bazza is most dismissive of 'poofs'. There is a long tradition of Australians ridiculing upper class English as effeminate, which recycles popular British mockery of its aristocracy. Humphries and Beresford indulge the old yobbo prejudice, while turning the joke back on the Australians who have great difficulty reading the sexual variety on offer. It is Barry's tragedy that his anxieties about women and his fondness for male company leave him exposed to several obvious 'pommy pervs'. Yet it is the handsome, beef-cake Bazza, dressing in a tight fitting stage cowboy costume to flog 'Camp Filter' ciggies, or donning the headmasters gown to oblige the masochist caning fetishist Mr Gort with six of the best who comes across as a bit queer. Barry's blind loyalty to his mates, and joy in being one of the boys—original larrikin verities—don't just exclude women but involve more than a bit of homosexual yearning.[27] Crocker is superb at camping up the confused machismo and sexual farce reigns as a dress-wearing Bazza is mistaken for a homosexual transvestite and pursued by a detective (Dick Bentley) through the underground. Even Edna isn't spared as she is seduced into a man's suit by the cross-dressing Claude whom she mistakes for a gent. In the best traditions of carnival much fun is had with the ambiguities of Humphries dressed up as a woman dressing up as a man, joining a masculine attired woman to 'dip into the well of loneliness'.[28]

While reminiscent of the sexual innuendo of the *Carry On* films, the light-hearted depiction of sexual non-conformity was bold for its sheer variety. Made before Monty Python's send up of an Australian university where the number one rule is 'No Pooftas', and a year before an openly gay lawyer became the hero of Australia's highly popular TV soap *Number 96*, Humphries and Beresford picked up on a deep-seated anxiety among true blue Aussie mates that social change was dragging things well and truly out of the closet. While Humphries, Beresford and Crocker were straight, they moved in entertainment and bohemian circles in which homosexuality was a valid sexuality, if one forced to speak in code. *Adventures* extracted comedy from male anxieties by appealing to the enjoyment of gender-bending burlesque among working class blokes, who made up the audience for the Les Girls club at

Sydney's Kings Cross and tuned in to laugh at footballers in drag camping it up on Rex Mossop's *Club Show* on the telly. A decade before Sydney would enjoy international celebrity for its Gay and Lesbian Mardi Gras, Barry McKenzie did his bit to free up the conversation about sexual diversity. Unfortunately the reconciliation to hetero bliss of Leslie and her weedy BBC producer husband Dominic (Peter Cook) is a weak and trite plot development that blunts the film's edgy play with sexuality. The radical (for the time) gesture would have been to leave Les in the amorous embrace of Claude!

The liberating and life affirming quality of *Adventures* is tempered by a nasty streak that is especially apparent in grotesque characterisation of supporting characters like the dysfunctional Gorts, the demented de Lamphrey, and the rapacious hippies. Revelry in the grotesque is a central element in carnival and Humphries' passion for it, indulged since his days as a student dadaist, emerged in 1965 in his first book *Bizarre*.[29] Full of illustrations of freaks and deformities and descriptions of perversions and deviant obsessions, he had intended this to be an antidote to monolithic notions of 'what is normal and what is not'. But for left critic Craig McGregor, it was evidence of Humphries' cynicism and 'fine nose for the cruel and bestial'.[30] For others, the grotesque can be subversive: *Adventures* helped shake up what cultural historian Geoffrey Dutton called 'the great Australian niceness' that had persisted from the interwar years into the 1970s. And for many Australians, it was not a moment too soon.[31]

Adventures took the Australian media by storm. Crocker remembers that '[a]lmost every day feature stories appeared in the nation's press, and stills of the movie were released to heighten the public's curiosity'.[32] There were posters of Crocker carrying bikini clad girls and 'Pommy Bastards' T-shirts. This novel publicity blitz hatched by Humphries was necessary as the film's distributor had rejected the completed film, with Roadshow's Alan Finney advising Adams to burn it. Adams hit on the imaginative idea of a selective release in independent cinemas, beginning with a celebrity bash at Melbourne's Capital Theatre for the premiere on Friday 13 October 1972. Outside the theatre, traffic stopped as hired protesters waving 'Ban Bazza' placards clashed with hired acolytes declaring 'Bazza's bonzer'. The audience loved it and word spread like patterson's curse. Roadshow, of course, saw commercial sense and *Adventures* hit the mainstream cinemas after all, enabling the film to go into profit and Adams to pay back the AFDC.

Not everyone was amused, especially not the critics, but most Australian audiences got the joke. It even heralded a new wave of larrikin films such as *Alvin Purple* (1973), *Don's Party* (1976) and *The True Story of Eskimo Nell* (1975). To this day Humphries takes great delight that audiences ignored the critics. For the moment the ocker tide was in, but it would turn, and Beresford, in particular, would feel the wrath of Australia's artistic elite. But in 1974, with Whitlam's cultural renaissance in bloom, it was time for Barry Crocker to wear the hat one more time in the big budget sequel.

2

Barry McKenzie Holds His Own

To my mind, *Barry McKenzie Holds His Own* is even better than the original. You know you're in for a treat when epic music and an interplanetary special effects sequence lampooning Stanley Kubrick's *2001: A Space Odyssey* (1968) tells you this is a Reg Grundy Production—no government funding criteria here. A grandiose swoop through the clouds for the opening credits cuts to a plate of live frogs being served on a French aeroplane—Frog Air—spiralling out of control because the pilot (Desmond Tester) is shagging the air hostess (Chantal Contouri). The first scenes take the imaginative leap of having Australian slang translated in subtitles—some of which are also in slang. The whole tone is sillier than the first movie but paradoxically Humphries and Beresford, who again shared the writing, honed a political satire audacious enough to feature Gough Whitlam in a cameo appearance. The film's overtly political edge is reflected in its pursuit of authority figures from police to ambassadors to dictators, but also in the mockery of fads obsessing the young cosmopolitan middle classes, and the sustained satire of 'The Australian Cultural Renaissance'. The colony versus mother country theme of the first film is

'You never knoweth the hour.' Edna Everage makes use of a Paris bidet to wash her smalls.

relaxed in favour of a wider spray, signalled by its location amidst the cafes and berets of Paris.

Where *Adventures* was faithful to the comic strip and had its feet planted in cinematic realism, the sequel exists in a parallel universe where anything can happen as it mocks the media landscapes of the time, jumping from Hammer Horror and Kung Fu movies, to espionage thrillers and boosterish government tourism documentaries. This genre-bending displays Beresford's postmodern talent for parodying different film styles and gives the second film more cinematic depth. The writing is superior too, combining the carnivalesque vulgarity and verbal jokes of the first film with a stronger narrative drive and better timing. Unlike the episodic comic book structure of the first film, this has a more conventionally structured story-line in which McKenzie is called upon to engage in daring-do in mock homage to British *Boys Own* adventure stories. The gung-ho imperial aesthetic is underscored by the title, and the new theme song, again by Peter Best, that parodies a Federation-era drawing-room recital.

Grundy provided Beresford with a much larger budget than the first film—$450,000 compared to $250,000—and it shows. *Holds His Own* was shot in widescreen Panavision on location in Paris and London with more lavish costuming, casting and a small army of extras. Beresford fills the frame with scenic vistas, action scenes and choreographed all-dancing musical numbers. In place of the sombre greys of Old Blighty in *Adventures*, Beresford's Paris is a city of light. Overall the film has a pastel palette reminiscent of Coles' New World cafeteria colour schemes of the '70s. Unusually for an Australian movie of this period, Beresford uses special effects like explosions, horror make-up, gun fights and even a parachute jump. Humphries claims that the budget enabled Beresford to build locations around a tour of their favourite clubs and restaurants in Paris. It is appropriate that a film that has so much fun exposing a gravy train of arts subsidies should have been wholly funded by a private company famous for its cheesy television quiz shows.

And the plot? Edna Everage, on tour in Paris with her nephew Barry, is mistaken for the Queen by two vampires, Hugo Cretin (Louis Negin) and Modeste Imbecile (Paul Humpoletz), who kidnap her to help lift the ailing Transylvanian tourist industry, located in a corrupt Eastern Bloc republic. Barry, his mates, some feisty sheilas and the governments of Australia and Britain must rescue Edna from the clutches of 'the illustrious socialist leader', Count von Plasma (Donald Pleasence), before he discovers Edna's true identity as an Australian housewife. On the way we encounter an ecclesiastic seminar on 'Christ and the Orgasm', Barry masquerading as an Arab to get into England as an illegal immigrant, a ghostly encounter with Barry's convict ancestor in a gaol, an immigration game show, a reprise of

Humphries's much spewed upon Jewish psychiatrist from the first film, and Barry's usual clumsy attempts to lose his virginity. Fosters lager has transubstantiated from the obsessive beverage of the first film into a magical potion rivalling Popeye's spinach, and Plasma is eventually seen off with a cunningly improvised cross of tinnies—the mighty Fosterix!

Bazza, Edna and their entourage of Fosters-guzzling compadres are led around the various tourist attractions of Paris by eccentric Australian expat, Col 'the Frog' (Dick Bentley). They are trailed by two vampiric and sleazy henchmen of Count von Plasma in the hope of kidnapping the Queen—but first they must dispatch Barry, who they mistake for the 'Royal Body Guard'. Their botched assassination attempts are interspersed with Bazza's confused misreadings of European culture. 'Cripes, Col', complains Barry, 'how can you live in this dirty old dump? Just a lot of old-fashioned buildings and not a decent beach in sight'. Culture shock takes a spiritual turn when Barry, masquerading as 'Kev the Rev', turns a religious seminar at Notre Dame into an hilarious song and dance routine about 'ratbags' that converts the congregation into raptures. Asked by an earnest social worker what he would do for a 'female parishioner with grave nymphomaniacal tendencies', Bazza replies that he would 'take her to the pictures, buy her a shandy, and then have a crack at putting the ferret through the furry hoop'. When a gay priest (Kevin Miles) wants to know where the Reverend McKenzie would place him in Australia, Barry suggests 'probably around Kings Cross in one of them all night dunnies'. Quizzed about the meaning of the Australian word 'ratbag' Barry and his mates launch into a song on the subject, ranging from alien abductees and 'people who think Shakespeare was a sheila' to Filipino healers. I love the irrepressible energy in the performance—especially the dancing by the Earls Court chorus—and the accumulation of anti-PC slanders, climaxing with Bazza admitting that everyone, himself included, is a ratbag.

Rarely has an Australian film enjoyed itself with such sublime nonsense. The idea of a Communist potentate as a vampire sounds laboured, but allows Beresford some fine Hammer Horror-meets-Cold War cinema parody. Edna Everage, while still a housewife on a package tour, assumes greater plot significance and in her masquerade as Elizabeth II hints at the purple-headed superstar to come. Barry Crocker reprises his portrayal of Bazza but also gets to play his twin brother, a with-it wowser clergyman the Very-Reverend Kevin McKenzie. The two get to appear simultaneously on screen and even have a seamlessly executed fight scene together. This time Bazza is less yobbo, more hero, sufficiently imbued with the Anzac spirit to find himself leading 'McKenzie's Marauders' in a paratrooper assault on Plasma's castle.

Holds His Own continues the practice of casting fine comic actors who bring a professionalism and sense of eccentricity to the supporting and cameo roles. Australian vaudevillian Desmond Tester is the wine guzzling, shagging French pilot of the film's opening. Arthur English from the camp TV sitcom *Are You Being Served?* is a pommy people smuggler who helps 'Abdul McKenzie'—Barry in black face, decked out like Lawrence of Arabia riding a camel—sneak back into Britain with a boatload of illegals. Deryck Guyler, the village policeman in the TV show *Sykes*, is a natural as an obsequious bobby teamed up with an Australian-hating Sergeant, played by another sitcom favourite, Frank Windsor, who is bitten by a snake charmer's cobra while arresting Bazza for illegal entry: 'Do you have a licence for that serpent, sir?' Cockney comic Tommy Trinder is Barry's spectral convict ancestor, 'great, great, great, great Huncle Harfur', who helps his nephew escape from an English gaol. John Le Mesurier, well-known from the TV comedy *Dad's Army*, plays the dapper English contestant in the immigration quiz show held at 'Oz House' that chooses who can migrate to Australia. In one of the funniest scenes in the film (one that takes the mickey out of the producer, game show king Reg Grundy), Le Mesurier is asked questions like: 'Which country leads the world with regard to music, opera, ballet, theatre, pomes, novels, paintings and fillums? You have ten seconds.' and 'Which country is the arsehole of the world?' Le Mesurier just makes the bell with an incredulous 'Australia' and a reluctant gasp of 'England'. There's a young, hirsute Clive James, an old mate of Beresford's, playing Paddy, a perpetually drunk expat Australian film critic, apparently based on the then European-based (and at the time left-wing) journalist Paddy McGuinness but doing a fair approximation of the younger Clive James. And the dad from *Skippy*, Ed Devereaux, resplendent in shorts and long socks as the Australian Ambassador, Sir Alec.

Best of all is Australian expat Dick Bentley, who had a trifling role as the detective in *Adventures* but now gets the meaty one of Col 'the Frog' Lucas. Col is a lefty/arty type living in self-imposed exile in Paris who has gone native—he carries a French loaf, wears a beret and two-tone brogues and can speak the local lingo ('Too flambé right!')—and who moonlights as a pimp and communist spy.[33] Described by Crocker as 'laconic as a cocky in country pub', Bentley, a doyen of Australian and British show biz, brought a jaded gravitas to the role.[34] Col is an

'Too flambé right.' Barry with his guide to Paris, Col 'the Frog' Lucas (Dick Bentley).

enigmatic character—a bohemian refugee from the 'internationally envied Sydney push' (according to the photoplay)[35] and a 'bit of an old bludger'. His moral laxity is forgiven by the 'clean living' Aussie travellers because he can charm Edna with his 'gift of tongues' and knows how to show the boys a good time. Col is Barry's guide, Virgil-style, to Paris, showing him Sacre Coeur, the Eiffel Tower, and an eighteenth-century style sado-masochistic striptease ('a bloody good cultural show') starring Nerida (Little Nell), Bazza's old Bondi girlfriend and expat 'comptometrist' gone bad.[36] When Bazza tries to rescue her from the 'mob of perving frogs and dagos' she pleads that a 'girl has to eat' while performing fellatio on a whip handle. Col tries to set Bazza up to lose his cherry with the 'convent educated' prostitute Germaine (a joke reference to Germaine Greer?) but when the nervous Bazza bolts, Col emerges from behind a curtain to collect his money, accompanied by melancholy French accordion music. Humphries enjoys contrasting the naïve McKenzie with Col's pretension to a European bohemianism that has succumbed to the moral swamp of Old World decadence and Harry Lime style double-dealing. 'I couldn't lie straight in bed', 'Comrade' Lucas confesses to Barry when his identity as a 'commo' agent is revealed. Col is a weather-beaten father-figure offering sage advice on life gone wrong, including Humphries' favourite dialogue about an unfaithful girlfriend who broke his heart:

> Col: I would have crawled half a mile over broken glass just to hear that little sheila piss into an empty jam tin.
>
> Bazza: Geez Col. Did she know you felt like that?

Beresford litters the film with visual gags: Barry, his suit lined with row upon row of Fosters Tubes, literally blowing up the Paris airport metal detector as soldiers with sub-machine guns fire a hail of bullets at the foaming cans, mistaken for 'some kind of Molotov cocktail'; Barry 'crying Ruth' off the top of the Eiffel Tower, but beating the descending chunder down to the ground, leaving the two villains to marvel at the gravity-defying physics and cop a steaming eyeful; a BBQ in Australia House with real Aussie travellers singing 'Bound for Botany Bay'; Edna Everage's narration of her super-8 film of Australia which climaxes in a blood drenched attack of sea wasps on Bondi Beach, to the delight of the lip smacking vampires of the

Transylvanian Tourist Commission; the kung-fu fight between Plasma's Chinese chef and the hapless Australians, delivered as a perfect homage to Bruce Lee with fast motion cinematography and guttural sound effects all Australianised with a disabling Fosters spray.

Holds His Own is gross, rude and offensive. Barry chunders twice, slips on 'an alsation's visiting card', tells a prostitute he's 'that randy he could root the hair on a barber shop floor', and poses nude for a *Cleo*–style centrefold for *Jet Set* ('the women's magazine with balls') with only an ejaculating can of Fosters to protect his modesty. As with *Adventures* the film's ribald antics turn upside down the stitched-up hierarchies of a string of condescending authority figures but the chief target is the hype surrounding the so-called 'Australian Cultural Renaissance' associated with the Whitlam Government, giving the film a hard political edge.

Holds His Own's play with the cultural strut packed a satirical punch for '70s audiences. While both films aim their satire at boorish post-war suburban males, the sequel goes after the new educated middle class that was taking on airs and graces in the wake of the 'new Nationalism' ignited by the patronage of Prime Ministers John Gorton and Gough Whitlam. Everyone is on the 'cultural' bandwagon. 'The Government's shelling out piles of bloody moolah on any prick who reckons he can paint pitchers, write pomes or make flaming fillums' Barry tells Col, explaining how drunken film critic Paddy 'copped $20,000 to come over here to go to the flicks'. In the 1970s, trendies bearing cask wine and a fondue set made shrill claims about Australia's new-found sophistication, much to the amusement of Humphries. 'Back in Australia', Bazza says, 'we've got culture up to our arseholes'. In *Holds His Own*, cosmopolitanism happens in 'the contemporary Australian-Spanish style' and European culture is to be found at the Munich beer festival.

In the film's pre-title introduction by Labor Minister for Culture, Senator Doug Manton (Humphries as a prototype Sir Les Paterson), with a model of the Opera House in front of him, a huge Fosters ad behind him, and the buzz of blowflies just audible in the background, audiences are informed: 'The fillum you're about to see makes me proud to be an Australian.' The movie's send-up of heavy–handed government patronage of Australian culture still resonates, as debates about national identity and the 'Yartz' are constants in our political discourse, erupting in Keating's Creative Nation vision in the mid-1990s, Howard's backlash against the inner-city latte set, and perpetual angst about the local film industry.

The film's main criticism of socialism—that it empowers bureaucrats to regulate human creativity—sprang from Humphries' individualism and belief in the artist-hero which was translated into political conservatism; he was hostile to socialism, both as a theory and in its totalitarian practice in the Soviet Union. And Beresford brought from his exposure to Sydney's libertarian Push a hostility to authoritarianism and to the welfare state, and a scepticism towards the left-wing romanticism of the early '70s. Bazza's 'Pommy Bastards' t-shirt of the first film was now replaced with one emblazoned 'Commie Bastards'! Communists are depicted as corrupt parasites using Marxist jargon to defend their privileges: 'This is an insult on the Transylvanian working class', hisses Von Plasma when he discovers Edna is not Betty Britain. The communist leaders of Eastern Europe are vampires sucking their countries dry (literally). Given what we now know about Ceausescu's tyranny and his grisly end this portrayal was not too wide of the mark.[37]

Like many conservatives, Humphries slides his critique of totalitarian Marxist regimes into easy put downs of the broader Australian left and the Labor Party. When Bazza and his mates parachute into Transylvania they pretend to be students from the Bondi Organisation for Radical Education (BORE) who 'all think the sun shines out of Stalin's arsehole'. Like Sir Les Patterson, Senator Doug Manton is a philistine. The Government officials who preside as judges of the immigration game show at Australia House are caricatures of the fat, middle-aged blokes who run the NSW ALP's Sussex Street version of Tammany Hall. In *Holds His Own* the much-vaunted cultural renaissance is a con being spruiked by the same old Aussie blokes in shorts and long socks who always run this place, personified in Ed Devereaux's knockabout Australian Ambassador who confesses 'I won't say we don't pull a few swifties to pull the tourists with all that garbage about that flamin' joke of an Opera House'.

'The fillum you're about to see makes me proud to be an Australian.' Barry Humphries as Senator Doug Manton introducing *Holds His Own*.

But it's not just unsophisticated politicians and cynical bureaucrats who are in Humphries' and Beresford's sights. Every crank idea and trendy cause of the '70s cops a spray of

The Barry McKenzie movies both satirise and appealed to the left. Cover from Comic book collection.

the always-foaming Fosters. As Bazza puts it in the 'Ratbag Song':

> A ratbag is a sheila or a bloke
> Who's kind of funny,
> But who never sees the joke.

The song salutes a galaxy of ratbags, including 'anonymous phoners', 'sperm bank donors', 'poofta liberators', scientologists and 'everyone in Ireland'. Humphries was building on his mid-60s character Neil Singleton, a beatnik-bearded, left-wing pseudo-academic described by Craig McGregor as Humphries' 'most savage and most perceptive stage satire so far'.[38] We know we're taking no prisoners when Bazza bumps into Rhonda Cutforth-Jones (Merdelle Jordine), the black, posh-accented, feminist editor of *Jet Set*. Rhonda asks Edna if she's ever 'balled a chick', and Edna replies with a crooked smile that 'I may be old fashioned, young lady, but lesbianism has always left a nasty taste in my mouth'.

And what of the colourful racist invective thrown around with such redneck abandon, beginning with the continuous disparagement of the English? At a time when Australia was busily apologising for the recently ended White Australia policy, *Holds His Own* shows a bunch of white blokes terribly anxious about other races. Old prejudices were clearly dying hard if its Australian Ambassador can say to a Transylvanian who wants to immigrate:

> We don't want types like you undermining our wonderful institutions and unique life-style, crawlin' like termites through the fabric of our nation-hood. We got too many chink lovers as it is.

Despite having come from a country in the throes of a massive immigration program and a government pledged to land rights and a racial discrimination act, Bazza and his mates don't care much for 'abos', 'heathen chinee', 'yellerens', 'frogs', 'wogs' and 'dagos'. Bazza does not mince words when he stumbles upon an expensively couturied Rhonda Cutforth-Jones emerging from an airline toilet with Dr de Lamphrey:

Feminist magazine editor Rhonda Cutforth-Jones (Merdelle Jordine) tries to 'liberate' Barry McKenzie.

> How come a clean living Australian bloke like me cops so many knock backs, when a dirty, Ikey Mo type bastard like you cracks it for a knee trembler with an abo in an airborne dunny?'

Humphries' and Beresford's ockers play with the language of the streets and playground rather than the sanitised language of government tolerance programs. While still shocking to us today, in the 1970s one of the most popular British TV programs was *Till Death Us Do Part* in which the working class, East-end London bigot, Alf Garnett (Warren Mitchell), fretted about 'coons' and 'Pakis' taking over England. In the same way, Humphries and Beresford were satirising the prejudices of the old Aussies rather than contributing to them.[39] Humphries was never a racist but he was astute and honest enough to know that many in the Australia of the 1950s and '60s were. Rather than ignore or despair at it, Humphries picks at the scab of Australian racism, ventilating this running sore. Today, *Holds His Own*'s pre-occupation with borders, people smuggling, airport searches and migration control seems eerily topical. Given Australia's ritual outbreak of immigration hysteria and the rise and fall of One Nation, was Humphries too far off the mark in suggesting that decades of prejudice could not be eliminated overnight by government fiat?

Holds His Own mocks radical chic but Gough Whitlam is OK: 'I reckon the PM is that smart he could sell soap to the pommies' as Barry tells his auntie. To show what a good sport he is, Whitlam, the Pericles at the centre of all the democratic patronage mocked in this private enterprise-funded film, appears at its end to welcome back the Australian heroes and, improvising before the camera, regally 'dames' Edna Everage, who is now set on her trajectory to housewife superstardom.[40] Quizzed by television presenter Mike Willessee as to why

Australia's Prime Minister stooped to appear in this of all films, Gough deadpanned: 'Hasn't everybody held his own? I certainly have.' For Humphries, Whitlam's appearance was 'like a mighty chord concluding a work of symphonic music'.[41] As a sophisticated cosmopolitan, he was both attracted by, and cynical of, Whitlam's capacity to change Australia. Humphries had seen the 1950s and knew that a nation of rough-as-guts old-style politicians like ratbag NSW Premier Robert Askin and Federal Labor Minister Rex Connor couldn't be changed overnight by whacking 'Blue Poles' over the fibro.[42] There is some truth to *Holds His Own*'s send up of the fellow travellers who did well out of the Whitlam revolution. In his 1971 play *Don's Party*, playwright David Williamson, who had sympathy for the left, made many of the same criticisms about radical hypocrisy, the gap between political philosophies and personal behaviour, and the discrete bourgeois pleasures of selling out and settling down.

Humphries did more than poke fun at the left: for a decade from the mid '70s he sat on the board of the anti-communist magazine *Quadrant* which then, as now, favoured the 'free market' while disparaging the '60s 'new class' of academics and protesters. A conservative contrarian while many in his generation were moving left, Humphries nevertheless retained a bohemian delight in transgression that makes him a radical. While Humphries the artist indulges elitist inclinations, the performer loves the applause from the crowd. Here was the paradox in Humphries' cultural politics, and possibly his personality.

The Barry McKenzie movies laugh at the expense of the left and the post '68 counter-cultures, but they are also an affectionate tribute to Australian larrikinism and a permissive

'Commie bastard.' Bazza does Kung Fu combat with the 'courageous socialist' and chef, played by Meiji Suzuki.

art of shock that sat uncomfortably with the Liberal Party. Due to the influence of protestant moralism, and petit bourgeois derision of the modern art that Humphries held dear, few on the Australian political right appreciated the Bazza oeuvre. An unamused Liberal Senator George Hannan railed in parliament about $250,0000 of public money going to make 'a ghastly vulgar film'.[43] Traditionally the Australian ruling class had always been uncomfortable with larrikinism, associating it with Irishness and working class unruliness. With the exception of Prime Minister John Gorton, larrikins have been thin on the ground among Liberal politicians. Humphries longed for the leadership of a sophisticated conservative elite who preserved what was best from the past unencumbered by fads and humbug. He was not to find it among the philistines, economic rationalists and tub-thumpers of the Liberal Party, which is probably why he prefers the port-stained, over-educated eccentrics who spice up the British Tory Party.

The Bazza movies ironically found their biggest fans among lefties, the students and ALP types they mocked. Left-of-centre historian Manning Clark congratulated Humphries for 'catching a type Australians recognise, and are really proud of, and so barrack for him as they would for one of their football heroes, or Ned Kelly... I loved it'.[44] This left-wing under-taste was strengthened by the films' association with Phillip Adams, who was well-known as an ALP fellow traveller.[45] Bazza's pommy-baiting played up to a strong anti-English sentiment among some sections of Labor, especially among those of Irish Catholic descent and, following the Dismissal, the growing number of republicans. While Humphries cared little for the 'It's Time' euphoria, *Holds His Own* is umbilically tied to this particular period in Labor's history.

Humphries' promotion of the carnivalesque in Australian life was a natural fit with Labor—then the home of wags, mateship and the long lunch. The quickest of wits, Whitlam did not share the Liberals' prissy disdain of Aussie slang, famously lampooning Queensland Premier Joh Bjelke-Petersen as a 'Bible bashing bastard', and wondering whether 'double-headed fellatio' was available in Tasmania.[46] More laterally, he responded to conservative politician Sir Winton Turnbull's pronouncement in Parliament 'I'm a country member' with 'I remember'. (Think about it.)[47] In the 1970s the government was chockers with colourful characters who brought personality and a dash of the larrikin to government. The loud-tie and silver-tongued Minister for Immigration, Al Grassby, Rex 'buy back the farm' Connor, the beatnik-bearded Moss Cass, the quick-witted 'Diamond' Jim McClelland, and the dapper, street-talking young dandy, Paul Keating were all political heart-

'Barry. Australia is proud of you.' Gough Whitlam welcomes home an Australian hero.

starters after the grey somnambulists who ran Australia during the long Liberal sleep.

Within ten years of Gough's film cameo, Australia was to elect as Prime Minister Bob Hawke, a larrikin character highly reminiscent of Barry McKenzie and who held the Guinness record for sculling beer. And when Keating became yet another McKenzie-esque larrikin in the lodge, he was to cause an entirely Bazza-style furore in England by daring to touch the back of the real Betty Britain. Larrikinism made a come back in 2003 when the ocker maverick Mark Latham became Federal leader of the Opposition. But it was to be all too brief.[48] Perhaps it is no longer time for larrikins? Nevertheless, from an era which made possible a celluloid encounter between a Prime Minister and Bazza, I am left with the passionate belief that an authentic Australian leader, especially a Labor one, should be a larrikin to smuggle a sense of the carnivalesque—what Keating called 'Vaudeville'—into our otherwise materialistic politics.

3

The Ocker Mask

Australian artists have long been entranced by working class culture, as a source of human drama, and as a cause of and a butt for humour. The Barry McKenzie movies brought to centre stage a performance that bohemian artists of the 1950s had long rehearsed in the pubs of Sydney and Melbourne and toured abroad as 1960s travellers to critical acclaim. The ocker, like the bushman, larrikin and digger before him, emerged in a period of national questioning, when the old certainties were confronted with a new cosmopolitanism and accelerating social change. In re-working these national types for the 1970s, Barry Humphries brought a keen awareness of social distinction and an ironic amusement towards Australian provincialism, sharpened by his own life as a suburban child, a bohemian artist and an expatriate.

The Adventures of Barry McKenzie displays an interest with social class not usually apparent in Australian cinema. Parodying the nuance of status, accent, education, cultural literacy, hierarchy, snobbishness and deference is Humphries' forte, and one not to be sneezed at in a public culture which believes its own propaganda that Australians are classless. From his own childhood in Camberwell he was acutely aware of the condescension, philistinism and wowserism nestling in the Australian bourgeoisie. Humphries believes people are unequal but does not support making them more equal. He believes in art and by conceiving himself as an artist, imagines himself above the hoi polloi.

When Humphries the '50s university student took to a life of painting and acting, he found the perfect identity in bohemianism. His biography describes his entree into the student and artistic demimonde, first in Melbourne's artistic Drift, then amongst the libertarian pub philosophers of the Sydney Push. These were the same circles in which a young Germaine Greer, Robert Hughes, Clive James and Bruce Beresford drank, argued and shagged. Barry McKenzie, the back bar orator, owes something to the rambunctious 'beerhemia' of 1950s Sydney. But Humphries was even then a one-man show. He was too nihilistic for the Drift and too aesthetic and foppish for the Push. Neither a romantic nor a political radical, he combined the dadaist desire to shock and subvert with the dandy's ease of superiority and social climbing. He was particularly fond of the aestheticism of the late nineteenth century which emphasised a refined and distancing taste, and had its apotheosis in the British wit and playwright, Oscar Wilde, who provided Humphries with a model for the type of artist he would be.

Bohemians are déclassé and are very good at crossing over borders—of class, nationality, sometimes gender, because identity play is their stock-in-trade. A performer like Humphries allows the Elizabeth Bay dowager or Carlton academic to cross-over borders of class and taste, if only for one 'Nice Night's Entertainment' (the name of one of Humphries' most famous one man shows). The best bohemians make themselves a work of art, modifying their identities and performances to suit the audience and medium, balancing the shocks with the familiar. Barry Humphries made this his career.

Edna may have come from 'a middle income bracket' but her wayward nephew was explicitly working class. 'I'm just an ordinary working man, like you' he tells Earls Court slum landlord Spike Milligan. Bazza is a caricature of the middle classes' worst fears about working class male behaviour—he is perpetually intoxicated, obsessed with sex, has a broad accent peppered with slang, swears and engages in all sorts of vulgar bodily acts, gets together with his mates in a gang, is belligerent and gets in fights, he has leisure and money to burn.

The fun of the McKenzie oeuvre is that it plonks lower class Australian suburbanites down in the heart of the Metropolis. Humphries doesn't like the Australian suburbs. He began his satirical career in Australia in the late '50s making fun of what he conceived as their insularity, banality and philistine conformity. His mockery built on a long tradition of Australian artists and intellectuals disdaining the suburbs as compared to the cosmopolitan inner city enclaves where they lived. This line is contradicted by the host of creative non-conformists, Humphries included, who emerge from the supposed suburban wastelands. My own experiences growing up in suburbs heaving with human drama and creative potential yet stifled by class blinkers leave me amused by the Humphries' sharp observations and gift for irony but wishing he was more sympathetic to the eccentrics, subcultures and stirrers who actually dwell there. However, in the creation of Barry McKenzie and especially the two films, Humphries' better angels prevailed.

Part of his critique of the protestant middle class suburbs

'More please.' Spike Milligan as grasping Dickensian landlord.

in which Humphries grew up was the denial of pleasure. Barry McKenzie, on the other hand, lives for the pursuit of pleasure, symbolising the lower urges commonly associated with the 'lower classes': both Humphries and Beresford appear to have enjoyed unleashing Bazza's vulgar hedonism on the wowsers. While Barry McKenzie is undoubtedly a piss-take of a certain type of unreconstructed working class Australian, he is also Humphries' life-affirming revenge on the thin-lipped, small-minded snobs he grew up with, who can still be found waving a disapproving finger at the larrikin and the eccentric.

Something interesting happens with Barry McKenzie when he is transported from the open space of the Aussie suburbs to the great wen of London. Like many expats before and since, Humphries was disillusioned with the England of his dreams. In *Adventures* dotty dowagers peep from behind faded lace curtains and the greedy landlord rubs his hands like Uriah Heap. Cockneys are depicted as gelded gnomes, surly officials or thuggish gangsters, alternatively deferential and bossy. No matter their social position, the English Bazza meets, from Peter Cook's obsequious BBC producer to the customs official who rifles through his luggage, are conscious of their place in a pecking order that polices their every move. Not so Barry and his mates, who blithely crash into or through these barriers and, as a consequence, experience a social mobility which was a lucky reality for a fortunate handful of Australian expatriates in the 1960s and '70s.

Some Australian writers, painters, actors and journalists, like Leo McKern, Dame Joan Sutherland, Peter Porter and Sydney Nolan did remarkably well in post-war London.[49] This mobility was raised a notch in the 1960s when the number of Australians journeying to London increased with cheaper air travel and self-conscious Australian neighbourhoods arose. This was the moment the Barry McKenzie comic strip captured so vividly. What changed from the mid 1960s into the 1970s was that Australians in London built careers in the arts and media as 'Australians' rather than Austral-Brits, and made an outrageous show of it.[50] Humphries recently admitted that the invention of the Barry McKenzie character provided 'a good outlet for my Australianness'.[51] The larrikin Aussie performance given by those such as Humphries, Beresford, Rolf Harris, Richard Neville, Germaine Greer and Clive James had an exotic appeal in the cosmopolitan mix of the great metropolis but also gave these well-educated stirrers a democratic post-colonial edge to cut through the British class system.

McKenzie uses a more extreme version of the same trick, but is more a 'loaded dog' than pet Australian. At a toffy party in a scene in *Holds His Own* he deals with English condescension by singing:

> I hope your chooks turn to Emus
> And kick your dunny down flat to the grass
> I hope your balls turn to bicycle wheels
> And back peddle up your arse
> I hope every lah di dah pommy like you
> Get the trots when he swallows a plum
> Go stick your left eye in hot cocky shit
> And your head up a dead bear's bum

An Australian suburbanite in the heart of the Metropolis.

This isn't Victor Laszlo striking up a bar room rendition of the Marseilles to drown out arrogant Nazis in *Casablanca* but for any Australian who suffered English snobbery in the imperial centre, Bazza's song could feel that good.

Humphries and Beresford, having experienced expatriation, seem to want to have a bet each way with McKenzie, mocking his provincialism but also celebrating an ingredient missing in the English regardless of their background. The result is that British audiences can enjoy laughing at the Australians, and Australians can laugh at the English. There is a tone of triumphalism in Barry exposing himself on national television in the first film's climax. Humphries and Beresford seem to be saying 'so there' to the establishment for every petty put down they ever endured. But then a chastened Bazza sheepishly confides to Edna as he is spirited away in a plane at the film's end 'I was just getting to like the poms'. The Bazza films straddle the ambiguity of Australia's love/hate relationship with the English in the post-colonial era, when we were keen to assert our differences and independence but not quite ready to sever the ties and go our own way. They reflect a time, now passed, when Australia could only frame its distinctiveness in comparison to the mother country.

In exploring the fraying imperial relationship, the Bazza films re-work the Anzac legend, the founding story of young Australian innocents abroad, to resonate with the 'New Nationalism' of the 1970s. Barry himself refers back to both world wars using recycled clichés from Anzac Day like 'our superlative fighting men', and both films play on the idea of the young Australians saving the old country in their own incorrigible way.

The films' use of a spirit of riot plays to the Anzac legend's celebration of the unruly digger bucking against English authority popularised by official war historian C.E.W. Bean. The Anzac association is made explicit in *Holds His Own*. In the first half, Bazza's drunken tourist mates sample the delights of gay Paris in a manner recalling popular accounts of the carousing soldiers of the First AIF on leave in France. When Barry is tempted by a Parisian prostitute he refuses because 'I once knew a bloke whose uncle in the war went chockers with a frog and his nose fell off'. On the lookout for some colonials to send on a mission over the Iron Curtain to rescue Edna Everage, Sir Nigel of the 'pommy Foreign Orifice' asks for 'some young, intelligent, sober Australians' before modifying his request to 'some young Australians'. When the drunken Australians turn up at an airfield at night for their mission, he asks if the boys would like 'a few grogs before they go over the top'. As they run riot the Ambassador assures Sir Nigel, 'I think you'll find they have plenty of the old Anzac spirit'. As silly as the ensuing battle with the communist vampires is, a quasi-serious note is struck when traitorous Col the Frog dies saving his mate Bazza, and redeems himself with a deathbed speech that could have come from the bar of an RSL club: 'I was one of those who thought there was a place better than Oz

... tell all those long haired students and commo unionists from Col the Frog, Australia is the greatest little country on earth'. The ANZAC myth, while celebrating the democratic, levelling spirit of the diggers, was quickly coopted for conservative ends, and so it is here.

Col's death represents a rare moment of poignancy in the films because it deals with the themes of sacrifice and mateship central to Australian national mythology. The film doesn't let it go: at the Old Cock pub in the film's last London scene, Bazza proposes a toast to their fallen comrade, and geysers of Fosters fill the air. Col's flag-draped coffin is borne home to a hero's welcome at Sydney Airport and carried by his mates past the Prime Minister; the last shot is of Col's grave, a mound of earth under a blue gum next to a sleepy billabong, marked only with a baguette and a pair of brogues—his dying request.

Humphries and Beresford, with some help from Adams, caught an emerging mood in their generation of artists with the character of Barry McKenzie, helping to invent the 'ocker', a '70s manifestation of the Australian larrikin tradition.[52] By the 1970s 'ocker' had superseded the elitist putdown 'Alf', but unlike that colloquialism, came to be celebrated as a badge of honour by people exhibiting what was thought of as typically raw 'Aussie'—working class, rowdy or uncouth—behaviour, in part thanks to the McKenzie films although they never use the term.

This was a period of rapid change, as blue collar work made way for office work, more and more women entered the workforce, tertiary education expanded, social mobility increased and mass migration brought new diversity. Artists like Humphries and Beresford, writer David Williamson and director Tim Burstall looked on the disappearing Australian workingman with both satire and nostalgia to say things about a culture emerging from isolation. Bazza is badged as a relic from a bygone era by his double-breasted suit and especially his hat and set lose amongst the foreigners, artists, hippies, ad men and women's libbers who make up a changing world.[53]

There is not a new social movement of the '70s that Barry doesn't drive to distraction, reminding us just how incomplete these revolutions were, and how intransigent suburban Aussie manhood could be. Ocker characters lacked the cultural capital of the bohemian to navigate borders smoothly. Ockers like Barry McKenzie, Stork, Alvin Purple and the loutish labourites at *Don's Party* made a loud nuisance of themselves as they crashed though classes, genders, ethnicities and nationalities. They allowed a new generation of artists to identify with Australia while simultaneously mocking how incomplete was its cosmopolitan journey.

The ocker trend was loudly condemned by an older generation of Australian artists and intellectuals who had come down firmly on the cosmopolitan side in the cultural wars of the 1940s and 50s, and could not read the social satire in the new nationalism, dismissing ocker art as dumbing down. Max Harris warned fellow sophisticates of art and literary circles that 'manifestations like Paul Hogan, Barry McKenzie, Alvin Purple are merely surface reflections of a backward shift to uneducated attitudes ... [a] reversion to proletarian tribalism' that must be opposed in the name of civilisation.[54] Adams astutely countered that

> Australians will always need to make its larrikin films for the simple reason that there are a vast number of larrikins at all levels of our population, from parliament to working class pubs with no two of them quite the same.[55]

As screenwriter and critic Bob Ellis argued: 'A country can't mature until it has learned to celebrate its gaucheries'.[56] The

Barry McKenzie has some difficulty with a metal detector as he navigates the border into France.

avant-garde modernists of Harris' circle, such as the Angry Penguins painters and writer Patrick White, had explored nationalist themes, but in an elitist way. The new nationalist artists of the early 1970s were exploring identity in the popular media and with themes that resonated with the younger mass audiences. Through the ocker, younger Australian artists like Beresford, Humphries, Burstall and Williamson have a bet each way, making art that appealed to the public's residual hostility to intellectuals and artists, while inviting the more discriminating to have a knowing laugh.

Conclusion

Forgetting

The critical assault on the Barry McKenzie movies was savage. Ron Saw in the *Daily Mirror* moaned 'had it not been quite so tasteless I might have been ill'.[57] Predictably, the *Age* condemned the film for its use of the lowbrow comedy of 'burlesque', 'farce', 'slapstick' and too much 'tasteless ribaldry' and reviewer Colin Bennet complained 'If *The Adventures of Barry McKenzie* were not an Australian film, it would rate about as much prominence as a Carry On Aussie ... Bazza should get a Reverse R: Unsuitable for anyone over 18'.[58] The *Telegraph* pronounced *Adventures* 'The Worst Film Ever made' and the *Melbourne Observer* condemned 'This unfunny mess'.[59] Audiences, however, did not heed the critics' advice, and both films made healthy profits, *Holds His Own* grossing $1,407,000, which was significantly more than the original—perhaps due to its rating enabling hordes of teens like me to see it.[60] Yet the sequel failed to achieve the national buzz of *Adventures* and the knives came out. Unrepentant, Humphries haughtily accused critics of envy, reminding them that the Bazza movies were popular and made money, unlike many films by 'totally inexperienced young Australians' enjoyed by 'their friends and relatives, if not very large audiences'.[61]

A casualty of the backlash was director Bruce Beresford, who could not get work in the Australian industry for a couple of years because of his association with the films. 'I learned the importance of film critics', he later recalled. 'They do not decide the box office but they can make or break a director's reputation.'[62] This was confirmed by Phillip Adams who maintains the McKenzie films unfairly stereotyped Beresford a lightweight within the industry.[63] He resurfaced, however, to direct David Williamson's *Don's Party* in 1976 followed by a string of critical and commercial hits in Australia and Hollywood, eventually *Driving Miss Daisy* (1989) into the hearts of middle America.

Despite being a hothouse for young creative talent that would fertilise Australian cinema for decades to come, the reputation of the Barry McKenzie films suffered from the local industry's late '70s weariness with ocker comedies. In the wake of the critical and commercial success of the extremely 'tasteful' European art-style movie, *Picnic at Hanging Rock* (1975), government film funding bodies and many film makers moved away from urban satire to embrace period drama and the colonial pastoral aesthetic. Critics and bureaucrats were happy to dismiss blokey comedies as the industry's growing pains. With the cultural renaissance in full swing we had become, like Bazza in *Holds His Own*, 'all sophisticated'. Some directors continued to make in-your-face exploitation cinema in the '70s. Brian Trenchard-Smith's Kung Fu action adventure *The Man From Hong Kong* (1975), low-life exposés like Bert Deling's smack-quest *Pure S...* (1975), Don McLennan's sharpie coming-of-age flick *Hard Knocks* (1980),[64] horror shockers like Rod Hardy's *Thirst* (1979) and Richard Franklin's *Patrick* (1978), and Tim

Burstall's accomplished thriller *End Play* (1975) had box office success. Yet they endured critical disapproval from a film culture increasingly self-conscious about the artistry of Australian film. By 1979, when *Mad Max* roared into our cinemas in 'the last of the V-8 Interceptors', the gatekeepers and tastemakers were blind to its creativity, so obsessed had they become with nationalist paradigms and worthy bourgeois melodrama.

The about-face on ocker cinema is perhaps understandable. Out with the old and in with the new is the natural rhythm of both modern art and politics. Soundly defeated in 1975 and 1977, Gough Whitlam himself spent the latter part of the 1970s and the early '80s in the wilderness of public life, a forlorn figure at the Australian National University and then an exile in Paris at UNESCO. But Gough came in from the cold and was eventually afforded his rightful place in the Australian Labor Party pantheon and also as a living national icon. The movies were not so lucky. While Bazza is fondly remembered by baby boomers and older generation Xers, the films were not given the encore screenings or serious study they deserved. *Holds His Own* was especially neglected: disowned by its production house, denied both a TV and video release and left to moulder in the Grundy vault. There it remained in the darkness, a victim of its status as a privately financed film until the end of the century. Only in Australia would a high budget and commercially successful motion picture that featured a host of national comic legends and a Prime Minister be so forgotten. There was not even a copy lodged in the national screen archive.

How was it that such a popular and influential cultural phenomenon as the Barry McKenzie films could be so easily consigned to the past? The answer is that forgetting our films is the rule rather than the exception, and unlike the Americans we do not balance the hype of release with a perpetually recycled archive. Those critics, distributors and exhibitors who define the canon of Australian film classics beatified but a handful of films from the 1970s, and only these enjoyed continued public attention and television repeat licensing in the 1980s and '90s. So while *Picnic at Hanging Rock* (1975), *Sunday Too Far Away* (1975), *Don's Party* (1976), *Breaker Morant* (1980) and *The Chant of Jimmie Blacksmith* (1978) are all celebrated, films like *The F.J. Holden* (1977), *The Long Weekend* (1977), *Patrick* (1978) and the Barry McKenzie movies slid into history, out of reach of new audiences and future generations of young film makers. Australians blow loudly about their latest artistic achievement, piling on awards and patriotic reviews, only to consign them to the dustbin when the next big thing comes along, insecurely living in the perpetual present. Perhaps it is the lot of the colonised culture to forget its own creative past, while remembering that of metropolitan nations like Britain and the United States?

Remembering

Bazza's luck began to change in the late 1990s when postmodern retro sampling of the 1970s conspired with baby-boomer nostalgia to prompt a reappraisal of the McKenzie cult and some other gems from that era. But there was more to the renewed interest than just '70s cool. Within both popular culture and academia there arose an interest in the Aussie bloke from about 1995, akin to the concurrent wave of 'laddism' in Britain. Magazines like *FMU* and *Ralph* appeared and Westie films exploring working class male youth culture under pressure like *Idiot Box* (1996) and *The Boys* (1997), gave chick flicks like *Muriel's Wedding* (1994) and *Love and Other Catastrophes* (1996) some competition. Inevitably, progressive men and women tired of the neutered impotency of the SNAG (Sensitive New Age Guy) and rediscovered the larrikin twinkle in the eye. In the late 1990s globalisation's threats to homogenise or cosmpolitanise provoked an ethno-nationalist reaction, spanning the white Australia nostalgia of One Nation, the restyling of Lawsonian folkways by troubadours like Paul Kelly and the deliberate reworking of larrikin journalism in independent media.

I played a small part in the resurrection of Bazza's fortunes when in 1999 *Strewth!* Magazine, a satirical little rag that a small group of us founded to larrikinise in the *Private Eye* tradition, conceived the mission to spring *Barry McKenzie Holds His Own* from the vaults. With some strategic celebrity intervention from Crocker and Humphries, the people at Grundy were persuaded to dust off their mint Panavision 35-mm print. We executed a one night screening to time tunnel Bazza from the '70s to the end of the century. All that was needed was to book the Chauvel cinema in Sydney, lean on Fosters for sponsorship and get Barry Crocker back in his hat and on the media circuit. The night was a 'bloody good cultural show' as trouble-makers like Paddy McGuinness and Bob Ellis rubbed shoulders with show biz celebs and a smattering of cast and crew. But it was Barry McKenzie's night, as the incorrigible ocker mounted the stage and read a regal fax from Gough Whitlam that saluted Bazza as a long lost prodigal son. Crocker recalled in his big-hearted autobiography:

Barry McKenzie holding his own once again, and released on DVD with its original movie poster.

> I donned the Akubra one last time ... Maybe it was simply due to the good natured gathering that had formed for that one-off screening, but I hadn't heard laughs so loud in a movie-house in years. The political incorrectness that galvanised critics when the movie was first released now seemed innocent...[65]

The movie was as big a hit with the mainly twenty- and thirty-something audience as with those who had seen it the first time round, like Ellis who declared it 'a bloody masterpiece'. And so, in 2003, three decades after its first release, it was given a new life as a DVD with commentary by Crocker and Humphries. Far from feeling entrapped by his chundering alter ego Crocker sees Bazza as a life's work, arguing: 'Humphries created a character that became an Australian classic and I adore filling his shoes to rove along the sands of time in the eternal hope of leaving a lasting footprint'.[66]

What is the appeal of these movies today? In the irony and sampling within the McKenzie films, contemporary audiences can glean a foretaste of the postmodern aesthetic with which they are familiar from '90s American pop culture such as *The Simpsons, Seinfeld, South Park* and the films of Quentin Tarantino. In a wonderfully self-reflexive moment in *Holds His Own*, a character mocks Australians for making 'B-Grade Yokel movies'. Bazza shares parody and pastiche with a handful of other excessive and self-conscious films from the '70s such as John Waters' *Pink Flamingos* (1972) and Jim Sharman's *The Rocky Horror Picture Show* (1975). Bazza, with his working class swearing, vomiting and anarchic fun, was a harbinger of the punk iconoclasm about to spit and snarl on to centre stage in the UK. Humphries' fringe fascination with the grotesque anticipated British comedy hits like *Da Ali G Show, The League of Gentlemen* and *Little Britain*.

Where is the spirit of Barry McKenzie today? Ocker comedy never went away, but has not always been handled as deftly. Humphries believes that *Crocodile Dundee* (1986), the biggest grossing Australian film ever, ripped off the McKenzie concept, going so far as to suggest that his own ideas for a sequel where Bazza goes to New York may have leaked into the Hogan film. 'It's a petty artistic larceny which no-one ever mentions and only an old sour puss like me likes to re-iterate at every possible opportunity', Humphries explained.[67] It's impossible to know, though who can doubt that Barry McKenzie laid the ground work for audience appreciation of an Australian comic style

that had its global apotheosis in Hogan's knife-wielding innocent abroad. But Paul Hogan's character and film were Bazza-lite, lacking the intelligence and transgression of the Humphries and Beresford original.

Thankfully, the Bazza legacy passed to more worthy successors. The ocker mask has been worn with style since the mid '80s by philosophical sports commentator-comedians, Rampaging Roy Slaven and H.G. Nelson. In the early '90s Kamikaze-cabaret artists The Doug Anthony All Stars hitched vaudevillian song and dance to subjects like tabletop excreta and doggy style sex and saluted tradition by inviting Barry Crocker to join in with them on ABC TV's *The Big Gig*. When the Working Dog team who gave us the television series, *Frontline* and *The Panel*, pitted a family of lovable 'bogans', the

Kerrigans, against the big end of town in their feature film, *The Castle* (1997), they struck a chord in the Australian suburbs and attracted huge domestic audiences reminiscent of Bazza's hey day. And the Anglo-Celts lost their monopoly on larrikinism in the '90s when 'wog humour' emerged from the suburbs with the stage show *Wogs Out Of Work* followed by TV and film spin-offs including Channel 7's *Acropolis Now* and another popular movie where the naïve but vulgar innocent triumphs, Nick Giannopoulos' *Wog Boy* (2000).

The larrikin carnivalesque has thrived in recent years. Edna and Sir Les remain national treasures but the ear for accent and social nuance has passed to a younger generation. Perhaps the pious censoriousness of the Howard years has stirred our inner larrikin to life after all? On television, *The Glass House*, *Kath and Kim* and *Pizza* reinvent the tradition to probe society and make us laugh. While Kath and Kim have confirmed Edna's secret that women indeed rule the child-like men of the suburbs, they now do so not by shushing male pleasures but by out-ockering them. *Pizza* is even more firmly the heir of *The Adventures of Barry McKenzie* because, like Bazza, it has the power to offend and shock. Today a show about vulgar, sexually explicit, hip-hopping homeboys of Mediterranean or Middle Eastern appearance outrages middle class good taste—especially when they make Australianness itself ridiculous. The larrikin streak is in good hands.

The Barry McKenzie films had huge impact at the time of their release and have entered the national iconography but only as spectral shapes. Sadly, younger people might know that there was an Australian character called Barry McKenzie but few have seen the films. Why hasn't an ABC, sagging under the weight of British imports, brought us the world television premiere of *Barry McKenzie Holds His Own*? Few young filmmakers—even those who want to make comedies—have bothered to seek them out to study what made them work so that we can build on the past rather than re-invent the wheel. Given the post-Bazza creative work of alumni like Beresford and Humphries it beggars belief that the Barry McKenzie films have been neglected by critical film culture and budding filmmakers. Looking back over the Howard years of resurgent wowserism, social dislocation, credit addiction and the abuse of authority it is a worry how so few Australian films engage with the world around them, preferring escape into the quirky and the personal. In the silence of this lost opportunity the clever social and political satire of the Barry McKenzie films seem even more remarkable. 'It's Time' Bazza was saluted as a brave moment in Australian cinema.

APPENDIX

BAZZA'S LINGO

Barry Humphries recalls a befuddled bureaucrat from the Australian Film Development Corporation waving the film makers off for London at Sydney airport with an anxious plea that the Barry McKenzie movie not use any 'colloquialisms'.[68] The rest is history. Barry McKenzie's obsession with excretory and reproductive functions allowed Humphries to showcase, and even improve on, Australia's 'seemingly inexhaustible reservoirs of slang' for body parts and their by-products.[69] Humphries garnered colloquialisms from across the Australian social spectrum, including dunny walls, school yard banter and his own invention. He aptly described McKenzie's colourful argot as ' a verbal pastiche of the real and grotesquely imaginary'.[70] Bazza's passion for creative euphemism, and occasionally dysphemism, is demonstrated below in this list of terms and definitions for body bits, seepages and appetites culled from a glossary by Humphries originally published in *Bazza Comes Into His Own* and reproduced on a promotional 'slang card' at the height of McKenzie mania. Seeping into the Australian schoolboy vocabulary of the '70s, some of Bazza's lavatory lingo still refuses to be flushed from the vernacular. The author takes no responsibility for any lapse in lexical best practice—or taste—in the original. It all made sense in the '70s.

A Glossary of Bazza-isms

apricots, to go up to. Presumably a fructological metaphor for intimate sexual contact.

bang, to (like a shit house door in a gale) (see under **feature**). To spoon, or have a nice romance with someone, I suppose.

beef bayonet (see under **percy, John Thomas, donger, nasty, nunga, old fella,** etc.). The virile member.

beef bugle. See above.

big jobs (see under **choke a darkie**). Three times around the bowl and pointed at both ends.

big spit, to go the. To hurl, chunder or play the whale.

brewer's droop. Alcoholically induced impotence.
bugle duster (see under **snot rag** and **gollies**). Hanky.
call, to (to call Charles, Herb, Bert, etc.). To vomit, eg 'Fantastic party last night; I called three times.'
chilled chunder drops. A cold can of ale.
chuck, enough to make you (see under **chunder, technicolour yawn, hurl, play the whale, park a tiger, cry Ruth**).
chuckle, to. To laugh at the ground.
chunder, to. See above. To cry Ruth, Herb or Bert. To enjoy oneself in reverse.
circuit, to on the chunder. A pub crawl.
clam, to spear the bearded (see under **sausage**).
coo-ee up the old snake gully. Cunnilingus, I fear.
crack-a-fat. To obtain an erection, I think.
cream, to c. one's jeans. To be in a state of heightened sexual erethism.
cry Ruth, to (see under **hurl, chunder** etc.).
darkie, to choke or strangle. To defecate, I'm afraid.
date locker (see under **Khyber Pass**).
dip the wick, to. To feature or exercise the ferret.
donger (see under **John Thomas**).
drain the dragon, to (see under **point percy, syphon the python, strain the potatoes, water the horses, wring the rattlesnake, shake hands with the unemployed, slash** etc). To micturate.
dunnee (see under **throttling pit, slash house, thunder box**). Bathroom, W.C.
exercise the ferret, to (see under **dip the wick**).
feature, to f. with (see under **naughty**).
Flags out, to have the. Red sails in the sunset, to have the painters in.
flash, the nasty, to. To exhibit briefly the virile member.
freckle, up the (see under **date locker**).
fun bags (see under **norks, top bollocks**).
fur doughnut, date with a. Possibly a reference to imminent vaginal contact.
furry hoop (see under **snatch**).
gnawing the nana (see **nunga munching** or **blowing the beef bugle**).
gollies, king-sized green. Mucilaginous deposits of the nasal cavity.
gong-beater. An onanist or person hopelessly addicted to self-abuse.
horsecollar, hop into the (see under **furry hoop**).
hurl, to (see under **chuck, chunder, cry Ruth, Herb, Bert** etc.).
jerkin' the gherkin. Stropping the mulligan, rod walloping, twanging the wire.

John Thomas (see under **mutton, beef bayonet, beef bugle, sausage, donger, unemployed, snorker, tummy banana, percy**). Wife's best friend.
Khyber Pass. Arse.
knee trembler, to score a. An all but consummated, stand up, fully clad embrace.
laugh at the ground (see under **chuckle**).
length, to slip someone a. To fall in love nicely.
liquid laugh. The involuntary release of recently ingested refreshment.
lizard, to flog the. To commit onanism.
lunch, to open one's. Possibly to fart.
make love to the lav, to. To chunder intimately.
Mrs Palm and her five daughters (see under **jerkin' the gherkin**). A metaphor for the hand in all probability.
mulligatawny. Rhyming slang? In a state of heightened sexual erethism.
mutton dagger (see under **beef bayonet**).
mutton merchant. A sexual exhibitionist.
naughty, to have a. To dip the wick or to feature.
norks. Top bollocks or fun bags.
nunga-munch, to (see under **yodel**).
old fella. Percy.
parquet, to point percy at the (also **porcelain, pavement**).
pea soup, to park the (see under **tiger**).
point Percy, to (at the porcelain). To drain the dragon.
poop. Big jobs.
rat up a drain, a (see under **rat up a rhododendron, dip the wick**, and **naughty**). Usually referring to coitus, I fear.
rat up a rhododendron. See above.
rod walloper. A compulsive onanist.
russet gusset (see under **skid marks**)
sausage grappler. A rod walloper.
sausage, to sink the. To consummate a romance.
shag, to get a (see under **naughty**).
shake hands with the unemployed; shake hands with the wife's best friend. To urinate, perhaps.
sheets, to christen the. An undesirable, involuntary ending to a convivial Australian evening.
skid marks (see under **russet gusset**). Stains on nutchokers.
slash house. Urinal.

slash, to have a. To strain the potatoes.
sleeping fat. A mysterious term, possibly referring to partial tumescence.
snatch (see under **furry hoop**).
snorker, the wily old. (see under **John Thomas**).
snot rag. Bugle duster.
strain the potatoes. Splash the boots.
syphon the python. Wring the rattle snake.
technicolour yawn. Liquid laugh.
throttle one, to. To choke a darkie.
throttling pit (see under **dunnee**).
thunder box. Dunnee.
tiger, to park a. To deposit involuntarily the colourful remnant of a large meal upon an appropriate surface e.g. carpet, bedspread, dining table, etc.
toms, the. The threepenny bits, diarrhoea.
top bollocks (see under **norks**).
trouser snake, one-eyed (see under **ferret, John Thomas**, etc.).
tummy banana (see under **John Thomas, beef bayonet**, etc.).
twang the wire, to. To jerk the gherkin.
Twyfords, to train Terence at the (see under **parquet**).
voice, to throw the. To vomit.
water the horses, to (see under **drain the dragon**, etc.).
whale, to play the. To spout, in the manner of Leviathan, a jet of partially digested nutrient.
wring the rattlesnake, to (see under **drain the dragon**, etc.).
'Y', dining at the (Y.M.C.A.) (see under **yodel up the valley**). Eating the old hare pie and tucking into a nice fresh furburger.
yodel, to (see under **chunder**).
yodel up the valley (see under **'Y', dining at the**).

Abridged from Barry Humphries, *Bazza Comes Into His Own*, Melbourne: Sun Books, 1979; Reproduced with the kind permission of the author.

NOTES

1 Reg Grundy was the Australian game show pioneer and the man who gave us *Neighbours*. Following the mainstream success of *Adventures*, Beresford worked on a series of documentaries for Grundy's including *The Wreck of the Batavia* in 1973 forging a connection that led Grundy to finance *Holds His Own*.
2 Beresford's film, *The End*, was presented as the work of Humphries' underground film-maker character Martin Agrippa in *Just a Show*.
3 Bruce Beresford 'Introduction' in Barry Humphries and Nick Garland, *Bazza Comes into His Own*, Melbourne: Sun Books, 1979, p. 3
4 Ibid, p. 4
5 Ibid, p. 4
6 These men went on to distinguished careers in the industry. McAlpine's DOP credits include *Don's Party, Breaker Morant, The Getting of Wisdom, The Fringe Dwellers, Clear and Present Danger, William Shakespeare's Romeo + Juliet* and *Moulin Rouge*; Anderson's editing credits include *Don's Party, Breaker Morant, The Getting of Wisdom, Gallipoli* and *The Club*. Best's scores include *Muriel's Wedding* and *Crocodile Dundee*.
7 Graham Shirley and Brian Adams (eds.), *Australian Cinema, The First Eight Years*, Sydney: Currency Press, 1989, p. 244. Nearly all of AFDC's investment was repaid within three months of release.
8 Colin Bennett, 'Starve the Lizards, Bazza's Up the Creek Without a Paddle', the *Age*, 13 October 1972. *Wake in Fright* and *Stork* were earlier films dealing with uncouth, vulgar Australians.
9 Max Harris, *Ockers, Essays on the Bad Old New Australia*, Adelaide: Maximus Books, 1974, p. 2
10 In the 1960s and early '70s children were warned to avoid 'dirty old men' with 'boiled lollies' which were poisoned, or 'baited'.
11 Barry Humphries interview with Mark Hartley, *Barry McKenzie Holds His Own DVD*, Umbrella Productions, 2003
12 Barry Crocker, *Bazza: The Adventures of Barry Crocker*, Sydney: Pan Macmillan, 2003, p. 362. Crocker was recalling the year of the film's release.
13 Peter Coleman, *Bruce Beresford, Instincts of the Heart*, Pymble: Angus and Robertson, 1992, p. 39. Beresford was DOP and Albie Thoms directed the actors in this 1963 student film featuring Germaine Greer among other luminaries of the Sydney Push.

14 This scene was cut from the televised version in 1975.
15 Crocker, *Bazza: The Adventures of Barry Crocker*, p. 360
16 Beresford, 'Introduction', p. 4
17 Barry Humphries, 'The Wonderful World of the Messrs Barry', in *Bazza Comes Into His Own*, p. 63
18 Barry Humphries, *More Please*, Ringwood: Viking, 1992, p. 18
19 Humphries, 'The Wonderful World of Messrs Barry', p. 63
20 Beresford, 'Introduction', p.4. Beresford continued to play with Australian slang to striking effect in *Don's Party* and *Puberty Blues.*
21 Humphries interview with Mark Hartley
22 In translating Barry McKenzie to the screen, Adams says they were conscious that 'Australian cinema has a larrikin tradition dating back to *The Sentimental Bloke*, to the early films of George Wallace, to the Dad and Dave series' and they believed it was worth modernising.
23 Lennie Lower and especially Roy Rene whose alter ego, Mo McCackie, featured in the comedy film *Strike Me Lucky* (1943) pre-figure the unconventional vulgarity of Barry McKenzie.
24 Author's interview with Phillip Adams, November 2004
25 Craig McGregor, *People, Politics and Pop, Australians in the Sixties*, Sydney: Ure Smith, 1968, pp. 32–40
26 The rock 'n' roll and jazz club where the Beatles performed in the early 1960s before achieving international fame.
27 Ross Fitzgerald, 'Bazza and Belushi–Lair and larrikin', in Clem Gorman, *The Larrikin Streak, Australian Writers Look at the Legend*, Chippendale: Sun, 1990, p. 157
28 The phrase refers to the novel of lesbian love, *The Well of Loneliness* (1923) by Radclyffe Hall.
29 Barry Humphries, *Bizarre*, New York: Bell Publishing, 1965
30 McGregor, *People, Politics and Pop*, p. 36
31 Dutton, Geoffrey, 'Australian National University Lectures 1978', in *Bazza Comes into His Own*, p. 82
32 Crocker, *Bazza: The Adventures of Barry Crocker*, p. 358
33 A parody of Alistair Kershaw, a supercilious, radical expat who forsook Melbourne bohemia for the delights of gay Paris where he worked as an ABC Correspondent. Barry Humphries, correspondence with the author, 1999
34 'Cocky' is slang for farmer.
35 Barry Humphries with Bruce Beresford, *Barry McKenzie Holds His Own Photoplay*, South Melbourne: Sun Books, 1974
36 Actor, tap dancer and singer

'Little Nell' Campbell who played Columbia in *The Rocky Horror Picture Show* (1975), and later ran a nightclub called Nell's in New York in the '90s.

37 Nicholae Ceausescu was the Communist dictator of Romania from 1967 to 1989. His despotic misrule led to the deaths of thousands of his countrymen.

38 McGregor, *People, Politics and Pop*, p. 39

39 Phillip Adams argued against the racial hatred legislation going through Federal Parliament in 1994. Rather than suppress racist language so that it festers, better to let it out in the open where it can be critiqued, opposed and, best of all, ridiculed.

40 Humphries, *More Please*, p. 305

41 Barry Humphries, 'Mussolini Paved the Way', *Bulletin*, 21 December 1974

42 Robert Askin was the coarse Liberal Premier of NSW notorious for greeting anti-Vietnam War protesters with the advice to his driver 'run the bastards over'. R.F.X. Connor was the old-style Whitlam Minister for Minerals and Energy whose Chifley-ite scheme to 'buy back the farm' became mired in a 'Loans Affair' to borrow Arab petrodollars for Australia from a shady middle man. In 1973 Whitlam weathered a philistine backlash when his government purchased Jackson Pollack's 'Blue Poles' for the National Gallery.

43 Quoted in the *Age*, 15 March 1973, in *Bazza Comes into His Own*, p. 76

44 Manning Clark, 'Letter to Barry Humphries', 16 October 1972, in *Bazza Comes into His Own*, p. 73

45 *Age*, 15 March 1973, in *Bazza Comes into His Own*, p. 76. During the 1960s Adams made the not-so-long march from Marxism to the Labor Party, from *Tribune* to the *Australian*. The vigilant Senator Hannan smelt a shady plot in Bazza's funding and asked parliament whether Adams was one of the ALP's publicity officers at the 1972 election—not realising that the AFDC funded *Adventures* under the McMahon Government.

46 Barry Cohen, *Life With Gough*, St Leonards: Allen and Unwin, 1996, pp. 52–53, 205. The Tasmanian remark was made during the 1970 Senate election and reported by Mungo MacCallum.

47 Whitlam Papers at www.whitlam.org/collection/2001/200105_Leadership _Material/

48 Mark Latham led from December 2003 until January 2005.

49 Stephen Alomes, *When London Calls: The Expatriation of Australian Creative Artists to*

Britain, Oakley: Cambridge University Press, 1999

50 Richard White, 'Cooee Across the Strand, Australian Travellers in London and the Performance of National Identity', in *Australian Historical Studies*, 116, 2001, p. 112

51 Humphries interview with Mark Hartley.

52 By the late 1960s the slang term 'ocker' had gained currency and was popularised as the name of a beer-swilling working class caricature on television's *The Mavis Bramston Show*. Its origins go back to the 1920s to a character in the comic strip *Ginger Meggs* called 'Ocker Stevens'. Initially, it was the nickname for anyone surnamed Stevens and the abbreviation for 'Oscar'. Prototype ockers appeared in *They're a Weird Mob* and *Wake in Fright* and in the television comedy series, *My Name's McGooley, What's Yours?*.

53 Tom O'Regan, 'Australian film in the 1970s: The Ocker and the Quality Film', Australian Film in the Reading Room, wwwmcc.murdoch.edu.au/ReadingRoom/film/1970s.html

54 Max Harris, *Ockers: Essays on the Bad Old New Australia*, Adelaide: Maximus Books, 1974, pp. 3, 10

55 Phillip Adams, in the *Age*, 1974, in Harris, *Ockers: Essays on the Bad Old New Australia*, p. 36

56 Bob Ellis, paraphrased by Phillip Adams, in Harris, *Ockers: Essays on the Bad Old New Australia*, p. 34

57 Ron Saw, 'Bazza McKenzie Makes Me Want to Chunder', in *Daily Mirror*, 12 October 1972, in *Bazza Comes into His Own*, p. 8

58 Colin Bennet, 'Starve the Lizard', in the *Age*, 13 October, 1972

59 Crocker, *Bazza: The Adventures of Barry Crocker*, p. 361

60 Figures sourced from the Australian Film Commission

61 Humphries, 'Mussolini Paved the Way', p. 79

62 Bruce Beresford, quote in Peter Coleman, *Bruce Beresford*, p. 61

63 Author interview with Phillip Adams

64 Sharpies were the 1970s Aussie version of skinheads, who favoured a shorn mullet style and loved the hard rock of early AC/DC rather than right wing politics.

65 Crocker, *Bazza: The Adventures of Barry Crocker*, p. 396

66 ibid p. 397

67 Barry Humphries correspondence with the author, 1999

68 Barry Humphries, telephone interview with the author, 2005.

69 Barry Humphries, 'The Wonderful World of the Messrs Barry', in *The Sunday Review*, 24 January 1972, in *Bazza Comes Into His Own*, p. 63

70 ibid, p. 63

BIBLIOGRAPHY

Alomes, Stephen, *When London Calls: The Expatriation of Australian Creative Artists to Britain*, Oakley: Cambridge University Press, 1999

Bakhtin, Mikhail, *Rabelais and His World*, trs. Helene Iswolsky, Bloomington: Indiana University Press, 1984

Bean, C.E.W., *Official History of Australia in the War of 1914–1918*, Volumes 1 and 2, St Lucia: University of Queensland Press, 1981

Cohen, Barry, *Life With Gough*, St Leonards: Allen and Unwin, 1998

Coleman, Peter, *Bruce Beresford: Instincts of the Heart*, Pymble: Angus and Robertson, 1992

Crocker, Barry, *Bazza: The Adventures of Barry Crocker*, Sydney: Pan Macmillan, 2003

Docker, John, *Postmodernism and Popular Culture: A Critical History*, Oakley: Cambridge University Press, 1994

Gorman, Clem, *The Larrikin Streak, Australian Writers Look at the Legend*, Chippendale: Sun, 1990

Harris, Max, *Ockers: Essays on the Bad Old New Australia*, Adelaide: Maximus Books, 1974

Humphries, Barry, *Bizarre*, New York: Bell Publishing, 1965

Humphries, Barry, *Bazza Comes Into His Own*, Melbourne: Sun Books, 1979

Humphries, Barry, and Garland, Nicholas, *The Complete Barry McKenzie*, St Leonards: Allen and Unwin, 1988

Humphries, Barry, *More Please*, Ringwood: Viking, 1992

Humphries, Barry, *My Life as Me: A Memoir*, Ringwood: Viking, 2003

Pike, Andrew and Cooper, Ross, *Australian Film, 1900–1977: A Guide to Feature Film Production*, South Melbourne: Oxford University Press, 1998

McGregor, Craig, *People Politics and Pop, Australians in the Sixties*, Sydney: Ure Smith, 1968

O'Regan, Tom, 'Australian Film in the 1970s: The Ocker and the Quality Film', Australian Film in the Reading Room, wwwmcc. murdoch.edu.au/Reading Room/film/1970s.html

Shirley, Graham, and Adams, Brian, eds., *Australian Cinema, The First Eight Years*, Paddington: Currency Press, 1989

N. Waterlow (ed. and curator), *Larrikins in London, An Australian Presence in 1960s London, Exhibition and Catalogue*, Paddington: UNSW College of Fine Arts, 2003

R. White, Richard, 'Cooee Across the Strand: Australian Travellers in London and the Performance of National Identity', in *Australian Historical Studies*, 116, 001

FILMOGRAPHY

Alvin Purple, Tim Burstall, 1973
Bliss, Ray Lawrence, 1985
Breaker Morant, Bruce Beresford, 1980
The Canterbury Tales, Paolo Pasolini, 1971
Carry On series, various directors, 1958–1978
Casablanca, Michael Curtiz, 1942
The Castle, Rob Sitch, 1997
The Chant of Jimmie Blacksmith, Fred Schepisi, 1978
Clear and Present Danger, Phil Noyce, 1994
Crocodile Dundee, Peter Faiman, 1986
The Decameron, Paolo Pasolini, 1970
Don's Party, Bruce Beresford, 1976
Driving Miss Daisy, Bruce Beresford, 1989
End Play, Tim Burstall, 1976
The F.J. Holden, Mike Thornhill, 1977
The Fringe Dwellers, Bruce Beresford, 1986
The Getting of Wisdom, Bruce Beresford, 1977
Hammer Horror series, various directors, 1957–75
Hard Knocks, Don McLennan, 1980
Gallipoli, Peter Weir, 1981
It Droppeth as the Gentle Rain, Albie Thoms, 1963
It Isn't Done, Ken Hall, 1937
Long Weekend, Colin Eggleston, 1979
Love and Other Catastrophes, Emma-Kate Croghan, 1996
Mad Max, George Miller, 1979
The Man from Hong Kong, Brian Trenchard-Smith, 1975
Mr. Smith Goes to Washington, Frank Capra, 1939
Muriel's Wedding, P. J. Hogan, 1994
Ninotchka, Ernst Lubitsch, 1939
Patrick, Richard Franklin, 1978
Picnic at Hanging Rock, Peter Weir, 1975
Pink Flamingos, John Waters, 1972
Puberty Blues, Bruce Beresford, 1981
Pure S..., Bert Deling, 1975
The Rocky Horror Picture Show, Jim Sharman, 1975
The Sentimental Bloke, Raymond Longford, 1919
The Sound of Music, Robert Wise, 1965
Stork, Tim Burstall, 1971
Strike Me Lucky, Ken Hall, 1934
Sunday Too Far Away, Ken Hannam, 1975
They're a Weird Mob, Michael Powell, 1966
The Third Man, Carol Reed, 1949
Thirst, Rod Hardy, 1979
The True Story of Eskimo Nell, Richard Franklin, 1975
2001: A Space Odyssey, Stanley Kubrick, 1968
Wake in Fright, Ted Kotcheff, 1971
William Shakespeare's Romeo + Juliet, Baz Lurhmann, 1996
Wog Boy, Aleksi Vellis, 2000

Television

Australian and various directors unless otherwise indicated.
Aunty Jack, 1972 to 1974
Are You Being Served, UK, 1972 to 1985

Barry Crocker's Sound of Music, 1970 to 1971
The Benny Hill Show, UK, 1969 to 1989
Club Buggery, 1995 to 1997
The Club Show, ATN 7, 1967 to ?
Da Ali G Show, UK, 2000 to 2002
Dad's Army, UK, 1968 to 1977
Doug Anthony Allstars, segment on *The Big Gig*, 1989 to 1991
Flashbacks with Barry Humphries, David Mitchell, 1999
The Goodies, UK,1970 to 1981
Kath and Kim, 2002 to present
The League of Gentlemen, UK, 1999 to 2002
Little Britain, UK, 2004 to present
Love Thy Neighbour, UK, 1972 to 1976
The Mavis Bramston Show, 1965 to 1968
My Name's McGooley, What's Yours, 1967 to 1970
Monty Python's Flying Circus, UK, 1969 to 1974
Number 96, 1972 to 1977
On the Buses, UK, 1969 to 1973
Pizza, 2000 to present
Seinfeld, 1990 to 1998
The Simpsons, US, 1989 to present
Skippy, 1966 to 1968
South Park, US, 1997 to present
Sykes, UK,1960 to 1965
This Day Tonight, 1967 to 1978
Till Death Us Do Part, UK, 1965 to 1975

CREDITS

The Adventures of Barry McKenzie

Release Year: 1972

Key Crew

Director
Bruce Beresford

Producer
Phillip Adams

Written by
Barry Humphries, Bruce Beresford

Based on the comic strip by
Barry Humphries, Nicholas Garland

Director of Photography
Don McAlpine

Camera Operator
Gale Tattersall

Sound Recordist
Tony Hide

Editors
William Anderson, John Scott

Lyrics for
'The Adventures of Barry McKenzie'
'One Eyed Trouser Snake'
'Old Pacific Sea'
written by Barry Humphries
'When His Old Light Shines On Me'
written by Barry Crocker
'The Adventures of Barry McKenzie'
written by Peter Best
Sung by Smacka Fitzgibbon

Production Manager
Richard Brennan

Additional Music
David McKay

Music Recording
Bill Armstrong Studios

Dubbing Mixer
Phil Judd

Costumes
Jane Hamilton, Gerry Nixon

Production Secretary
Jane Scott

Casting Director
John D. Collins

Continuity
Elizabeth Honey

Props
Lynn Holms

Set Builder
Dan Bodie

Stills
Peter Harvey

Hairdressing
Susan Scott

Make Up
Anne Taylor, Penny Stayne, Helen Dyson

Titles
Fran Burke

Key Cast

Barry Crocker
Barry McKenzie

Barry Humphries
Aunt Edna, Hoot, Meyer de Lamphrey

Margo Lloyd
Mrs McKenzie

Wilfred Grove
customs officer

Bernard Spear
taxi driver

Paul Bertram
Curly

Spike Milligan
landlord

Jonathan Hardy
Groove Courtenay

Maria O'Brien
Caroline Thighs

Dennis Price
Mr Gort

Avice Landon
Mrs Gort

Jenny Tomasin
Sarah Gort

Chris Malcolm
Sean

Julie Covington
Blanche

John Joyce
Maurie Miller

Mary Anne Severne
Leslie

Judith Furse
Claude

Dick Bentley
detective

Peter Cook
Dominic

John Clarke
Australian painter
Brian Tapply
underground composer
Joan Bakewell
herself
and
Members of the Rickmansworth Players
Blanche Coleman and Her Girls
Mica Beach Aboriginal Corroboree Dancers

Barry McKenzie Holds His Own

Release Year: 1974

Key Crew

Director, Producer
Bruce Beresford
Original Photoplay by
Barry Humphries in collaboration with Bruce Beresford
Director of Photography
Don McAlpine
Editor
William Anderson
Production Designer
John Stoddart
Music
Peter Best
Sound
Des Bone
Sound Mixer
Peter Fenton
Art Director
Alan Cassie
Assistant Director
Neil Vine-Miller
2nd Assistant Director
David Barrow
3rd Assistant Director
Dick Berrin
Production Manager
Drummond Challis
Associate Producer
Jane Scott
Costume Design
Jane Hamilton
Editing Assistants
Ashley Smith, Andrew Stewart
Make Up
Chris Tucker, Bob Lawrence, Ann Taylor, Judy Lovell
Special Effects
Cliff Robertson, Nobby Clarke, John Evans
Title Design
Sandy Field

Key Cast

Barry Crocker
Barry McKenzie
Barry Humphries
Aunt Edna, Senator Douglas Manton, Meyer de Lamphrey, Offensive Buck-toothed Englishman
Donald Pleasence
Erich Count von Plasma
Desmond Tester
Marcel Escargot, Pilot
Chantal Cantouri
Zizi, Air Hostess
Louis Negan
Hugo Cretin
Paul Humpoletz
Modeste Imbecile
Andrew Lodge
Scrotum Baker
Clive James
Paddy
Craig Canning
Tassie
Michael Downey
Skeeter
Merdelle Jordine
Rhonda Cutforth-Jones
Dick Bentley
Col 'The Frog' Lucas
Nancy Blair
Clothilde
Robert Gillespie
Dorothy
Little Nell
Nerida Brealey
Katya Wyeth
Germaine
Barry Crocker
Kevin McKenzie
Beatrice Aston
Cherylene McKenzie
Michael Newman
Foureyes Fenton
Arthur English
Cockney People Smuggler

Bruce Beresford directing cast and crew.

Frank Windsor
Police Sergeant
Derek Guyler
Police Constable
Tommy Trinder
Arthur McKenzie
Don Spencer
Quizmaster
John Le Mesurier
Robert Crowther
Ed Devereaux
Sir Alec Ferguson
Brian Tapply
Sir Nigel Stewart
Lincoln Webb
Ambrose Cutforth-Jones
Meiji Suzuki
Kung Fu Champion
Gough Whitlam
Himself
Margaret Whitlam
Herself
Roy Kinnear
Bishop Of Paris
Kevin Miles
Homosexual Priest
Margo Reid
Noleen, Secretary
To Australian Ambassador
Gail Galih
Indian Girl
Julian Jebb
Second Offensive Englishman
Fiona Richmond
French Stripper
Philip Lloyd
Transylvanian Guide
John James
Transylvanian Waiter